WANTED

WANTED: the real identity of this man and the reasons behind his alleged activities involving the Mafia and the assassination of John F. and Robert F. Kennedy.

LEGACY OF DOUBT

by
Peter Noyes

PINNACLE BOOKS • NEW YORK CITY

To my wife, Grace, and our son, Jack, for their love, patience, and understanding. And to my mother and father for their inspiration and motivation.

PINNACLE BOOKS, INC.
275 Madison Avenue
New York, N.Y. 10016

ACKNOWLEDGMENTS

I would like to thank the following persons for their generous assistance and contributions, which were indispensable to me in making this book a reality:

William W. Turner, Bernard Fensterwald, Jr., Manual (Chic) Gutierrez (deceased), Matthew William Byrne, Jr., Paul Gaither, Robert Harris, Al Chapman, Keith Benet, Tom McDonald, Angus D. McEachen, Earl Golz, Sam Barrett, Robert Smith, Grant Holcomb, L. K. Jessop, Carolyn McCoy, Donald Shepherd, Jack Fox, and Canoy Crawford.

Also certain officers and agents of the California Justice Department, the Los Angeles Police Department, the Federal Bureau of Investigation, the United States Probation Department, the Los Angeles Sheriff's Department, the United States Internal Revenue Service, and the Crime Commission of Greater Miami.

Also two private organizations: Intertel and the Committee to Investigate Assassinations.

CONTENTS

Preface

THE LEGACY OF DOUBT

The assassination of President John Fitzgerald Kennedy in Dallas, Texas, left a legacy of doubt in the mind of every American who lived through those horrifying moments in Dealey Plaza. For a time, the very structure of the Republic seemed threatened.

It was inevitable that the question of a conspiracy would be raised. For a century there had been a cloud of controversy over the assassination of President Abraham Lincoln in Ford's Theatre. And there were those conspiracy-minded students of history who found dark parallels between the Lincoln and Kennedy murders.

President Lyndon Johnson was mindful (even fearful) of this when he asked United States Supreme Court Chief Justice Earl Warren to take command of a commission that would investigate the Kennedy assassination. Mr. Johnson knew full well that the credibility of certain public institutions had been challenged; that the invincible mystique that sheltered the FBI, Secret Service, and CIA had all but evaporated in the smell of gunpowder in Dealey Plaza on November 22, 1963.

These agencies, it turned out, were composed of mere mortals despite the Godlike qualities the public had been led to believe they possessed. Plainly put, the leaders of these governmental security agencies were men who put their pants on one leg at a time. They had failed to protect the President of the United States in the hostile political climate of conservative Dallas. To add to their humiliation and the subsequent erosion of public confidence in law enforcement, these same government agencies stood by, useless appendages to the administration of justice, while the embittered young man who was said to have killed the president was publicly executed by a small-time thug, live on television. No one who lived through it will ever forget the horror that was Dallas.

In appointing a blue-ribbon group of public officials and some of the country's most distinguished lawyers to the Warren Commission, Mr. Johnson clearly hoped to demonstrate to the American people that the truth would make them whole again. Lyndon Johnson was keenly aware of the climate of hate scorching the country at the time John Kennedy was murdered, and he also realized that among the haters were those who were lurking in the shadows just waiting to jump at the first opportunity to accuse him of complicity in the assassination.

So what was the end result? After the most extensive criminal investigation in history, the

Warren Commission ruled that, based on the evidence available, Lee Harvey Oswald was a solitary killer and that he alone was responsible for the death of the thirty-fifth President of the United States.

The release of the Warren Commission's findings in September of 1964 was instantly hailed by most of the American press as a verdict above reproach. At that citadel of contemporary journalism, the *New York Times*, the distinguished Harrison E. Salisbury wrote: "The quest for truth has been long and arduous." Salisbury suggested that those who challenged the official investigation did so for self-serving reasons.

He continued, "Around the death of Mr. Kennedy has sprung up a mystique. In part it is a mystique of the martyr. In part it derives special appeal from the dead President's youth and vitality. And in part it is the deliberate product of widely differing political forces and tendencies— including tendencies of dangerous implication to the American system."

The *New York Times* and Harrison E. Salisbury obviously would not be partners to the type of skepticism that became so pronounced in 1973 when the Watergate scandal became a *cause célèbre* in that newspaper.

Salisbury wrote, "Out of this situation a hundred theories have burgeoned as to how and why the President was killed. It is safe to predict that another hundred will spring up."

Simply stated, the Warren Report was an official government verdict, and the willingness of so many people to take it at face value was symptomatic of that period.

Nonetheless, what Harrison Salisbury wrote about the probability of a multitude of assassination theories evolving was indeed prophetic. They virtually poured out of the woodwork.

Attorney Mark Lane was the first man to challenge seriously the findings of the Warren Commission. His book *Rush to Judgment* climbed spectacularly to the top of the best-seller lists. Lane set himself up as a lawyer trying to defend Lee Harvey Oswald, and indeed his challenge to the Warren Commission was compelling, although he failed to present any new evidence that could possibly alter the conclusion that Oswald acted alone. Numerous other books followed in both the United States and Europe. Perhaps one of the more intriguing was the work of Professor Richard Popkin who advanced the theory that there were two Oswalds operating in Dallas at the time of the assassination—one who could drive a car, another who couldn't. Indeed, Oswald's movements on November 22, 1963, would seem to give credence to the Popkin theory.

Then, too, there were the underground newspapers, which never let their readers forget the JFK assassination. More often than not they contributed to the legacy of doubt by blaming the assassination on the establishment—in most cases the FBI or the CIA.

Chief Justice Earl Warren didn't do his own

commission any favors when he advised the American people that the truth about the assassination might not be known in their "lifetime." It was not a facetious remark by the now retired Chief Justice. It was his belief that the commission, with all its enormous resources, had rendered the best possible verdict under the circumstances. But make no mistake about it—Earl Warren, by his own admission, was also an heir to the legacy of doubt.

Public opinion polls taken in 1966 and 1967 showed that most Americans shared the same doubts as Earl Warren; most believed there was a distinct possibility that John Fitzgerald Kennedy died as the result of a conspiracy. Then, when both Martin Luther King, Jr., and the slain President's brother Senator Robert Kennedy were assassinated back to back in 1968, the conspiratorial view of history almost became engrained in the mind of the American public. Hardly anyone was startled when James Earl Ray, a drifter and petty thief, pleaded guilty to the murder of Dr. King, then told the court he disagreed with those who said there was no conspiracy in the murder of the black civil-rights leader. At this point, who could blame the public for being numb?

In January of 1970 the late Senator Richard B. Russell of Georgia became the first member of the Warren Commission to take issue with its announced conclusion that Oswald planned and carried out the assassination by himself. But the remarks of the distinguished leader of the upper house did not even seem to tweak the thinking process of the dormant press and public.

Senator Russell said he was convinced that Oswald did the actual shooting in Dealey Plaza but that he never believed for a moment that the sulking ex-Marine masterminded the plot to kill John Kennedy by himself. Russell revealed that it was because of this doubt that he insisted a disclaimer sentence be placed in the Warren report before he would sign it.

That sentence says:

> Because of the difficulty of proving negatives to a certainty, the possibility of others being involved with Oswald or [Jack] Ruby cannot be categorically established, but if there is any such evidence it has been beyond the reach of all the investigative agencies and resources of the United States and has not come to the attention of this commission.

A short time after Russell broke his silence, the man who had set the machinery in motion for the investigation admitted that he too was heir to the legacy of doubt.

In an interview with Walter Cronkite of CBS News, former President Lyndon Johnson acknowledged that he had become addicted to the conspiratorial theory as it applied to that dark moment in Dealey Plaza. Specifically, Mr. Johnson expressed reservations and doubts "about the motivations and connections" of Lee Harvey Oswald. He said he was particularly disturbed by Oswald's relationship with the Communist Party. Unfortunately, the American people were never permitted to see that portion of the Cronkite interview of Mr. Johnson on television. Shortly before its scheduled broadcast on May 1, 1971, Mr. Johnson demanded that his critical comments about the Warren Commission's findings be deleted from the broadcast and left on the cutting-room floor.

CBS had paid Mr. Johnson $300,000 for a series of interviews to be broadcast on national television, and the suggestion that he had the right to exercise censorship over what he had initially said for the record was considered unthinkable by the news people responsible for the program. But in the end Mr. Johnson prevailed and his remarks were deleted. The official reason given by CBS for the censorship was "grounds of national security." But reporter Ronald Kessler of the *Washington Post* managed to pry loose Mr. Johnson's remarks about the assassination from sources inside CBS News, and the late President's doubts about the Warren Report were printed before the actual broadcast on television.

But once again there was hardly a ripple at the official level. Not one member of Congress asked for a reopening of the investigation of the President's death, and the late FBI Chief, J. Edgar Hoover, as usual had no comment.

Then in September of 1970 Senator George

Murphy of California, campaigning for reelection, announced that he too was an heir to the legacy of doubt, but his reasons seemed to be somewhat different from those of Lyndon Johnson. Speaking in the northern California town of Fremont, Murphy—a Republican and former movie star—startled his conservative audience when he said it was his opinion that the killers of both John and Robert Kennedy may have acted under orders from someone else.

Murphy said, "A President and his brother have been assassinated, for what reason and by whose order I'm still not certain."

After the speech reporters asked Murphy to elaborate on his remarks concerning the two assassinations, but the Senator declined, saying there would be no more discussion of the subject.

I knew Murphy personally, and I decided to press for a more comprehensive explanation. But the Senator was reluctant to produce any additional details, and his aides were likewise reluctant to talk, which led me to believe that there may indeed have been some substance—above and beyond political rhetoric—to his remarks in Fremont. Then, at a chance meeting at the Los Angeles Hall of Justice with Chief Deputy District Attorney John Howard, the man who successfully prosecuted Senator Robert Kennedy's killer, Sirhan Bishara Sirhan, I was able to obtain some insight into the motivation behind Senator George Murphy's speech. One of Murphy's aides suddenly entered the room, and with John Howard asking the questions, we learned that at that very moment, top secret hearings concerning the assassinations of both John and Robert Kennedy were in progress in Washington before the Senate Judiciary Committee. The aide said the committee was hearing testimony from several crucial witnesses to both assassinations. There is no public record of such a hearing taking place in the fall of 1971. But in fact it did take place, at a location far removed from the regular hearing room where Senator William Eastland presided over the Judiciary Committee. Furthermore, an aide to the senior Senator from Mississippi told me that three of the committee's staff investigators had been searching for information in the Los Angeles area —information about the two Kennedy assassinations.

But if the Senate Judiciary Committee and its investigators produced anything in the way of evidence that might remotely suggest a conspiracy in either assassination, it has never come to the attention of the American public.

For some time, in the normal course of covering the news, I had been gathering shreds of evidence about the two assassinations. But quite honestly, I did not initially share in the legacy of doubt. Like most other newsmen, I was content with the findings of the Warren Commission—even more so after Ealing "Jim" Carrouthers Garrison, the District Attorney of New Orleans, insulted the intelligence of the American public with his disastrous investigation into the assassination of John Kennedy.

But the doubts expressed by Lyndon Johnson, Richard Russell, and Earl Warren, plus what I had learned from the Senate Judiciary Committee and from Washington newspaper reporters who covered the United States Justice Department, led me to the conclusion that I should carefully examine the shreds of evidence in my possession and conduct a personal investigation of John Kennedy's assassination in Dallas. At first glance such a suggestion undoubtedly seems ludicrous in view of the vast resources of the federal government. My personal research convinced me there was no deceit in the Warren Report; no attempt to mislead historians. It appeared to me to be an honest compilation of both fact and trivia.

Those who slash away at the credibility of the Warren Report never seem able to produce one iota of evidence that would stand up in a court of law. If there were any mistakes reflected in the Warren Report (and I am convinced there were without suggesting they were proof per se of a conspiracy), they occurred in the investigation of what happened in Dealey Plaza in those fleeting, emotionally jarring moments after Lee Harvey Oswald, from his perch in the Texas Book Depository, fired the fatal rifle bursts that killed John Kennedy.

To explain why, it is necessary to begin at the beginning.

I

THE FACE IN THE CROWD

Within minutes after President John Fitzgerald Kennedy was slain in Dealey Plaza, Dallas, Texas, on November 22, 1963, law-enforcement officers rounded up a dozen or so men for questioning. Some were drifters and bums. Others were just plain, ordinary citizens who, for some reason, appeared to be acting suspiciously during that moment of madness.

Photographs of those scooped up in the Dealey Plaza dragnet show a man closely resembling James Earl Ray, who five years later would confess to the killing of Dr. Martin Luther King, Jr., in Memphis, Tennessee. But we are told quite explicitly that the man in the photographs couldn't possibly be the same person who killed the black civil-rights leader, since Ray was in prison at the time of the JFK assassination.

Another face plucked out of the crowd in Dealey Plaza seemed to be that of a most unlikely suspect whom the fates had unkindly placed squarely in the middle of the assassination.

When confronted by Deputy C. L. "Lummie"

Lewis of the Dallas County Sheriff's Department, this apparent man of means identified himself as Jim (no middle initial) Braden, and said he was in the oil business in one of California's more affluent communities, Beverly Hills. The man who called himself Jim Braden first tried to identify himself with a gasoline-company credit card, which made the deputy somewhat suspicious, since a driver's license is normally considered the proper way to identify yourself to a policeman.

So despite his protests the man called Braden was taken to the Dallas Sheriff's station for questioning by Deputy Lewis, who was one of the first officers to arrive at the Texas Book Depository after rifle fire from a window perch in that building snuffed out the President's life.

What followed is a footnote to history, obscurely tucked away in Volume XIX of the Warren report under the exhibit presented to the Commission by the late Sheriff of Dallas County Bill Decker, at one time perhaps the most famous lawman in the Southwest.

During the interrogation at the Sheriff's station Braden said that he was forty-eight years old; that he had been in Dallas for two days, and was staying at the Cabana Motel, on the Stemmons Freeway, a short distance from Dealey Plaza.

Deputy Lewis wrote down the number of Braden's California driver's license. He also noted in his report to Sheriff Decker that Braden "was in building when Pres. assassinated."

Lewis apparently satisfied himself that Jim

Braden was who he said he was. No fingerprinting was done. There was no check of criminal records.

Before being released, Braden agreed to make a voluntary statement, which eventually was included in the Warren report.

This is what the man called Braden said in that statement to Deputy Lewis:

I am here on business [oil business] and was walking down Elm Street trying to get a cab and there wasn't any. I heard people talking, saying "My God, the President has been shot." Police cars were passing me coming down the triple underpass and I walked up among other people and this building was surrounded by police officers with guns and we were all watching them.

I moved on up to the building across the street from the building which was surrounded and I ask one of the girls if there was a telephone that I could use and she said "Yes, there is one on the third floor of the building where I work." I walked through a passage to the elevator where they were all getting on [the freight elevator] and I got off on the third floor of the building with all the other people and there was a lady using the pay phone and I ask her if I could use it when she hung up and she said it was out of order and I tried to use it but with no success. I ask her how I can

21

get out of this building and she said, "There is an exit right there," and then she said, "Wait a minute here is the elevator now." I got on the elevator and returned to the ground floor and the colored man who ran the elevator said, "You are a stranger in this building and I was not supposed to let you up," and he ran outside to an officer and said to the officer that he had just taken me up and down in the elevator and the officer said for me to identify myself and I presented him with a credit card and he said, "Well we have to check out everything" and took me to his superior and said for me to wait and "We will check it out." I was then taken to the Sheriff's office and interrogated.

Jim Braden signed the "voluntary statement." It was notarized and then he was permitted to leave the Dallas County Sheriff's station.

Shortly thereafter the man called Braden flew to Houston, ostensibly on more oil business. From Houston he went to Louisiana, then flew back to California.

Two months later, on January 29, 1964, FBI agents Chester C. Orton and John K. Anderson visited Braden in his office at the Wallace White Investment Company, 215 South La Cienega Boulevard, Beverly Hills. Orton and Anderson did so at the request of the FBI bureau in Dallas, which wanted to wrap up any loose ends surrounding Braden's presence in Dealey Plaza on November 22, 1963.

The story Braden told the FBI agents was virtually identical to the account he had given Deputy Lewis in Dallas, with this amplification: "Braden," the official FBI report noted, "has no information concerning the assassination and both Lee Harvey Oswald and Jack Ruby are unknown to him."

Superficially, at least, it appeared to be a plausible story, and that was the end of the investigation. The agents took Braden at his word when he said he was not familiar with Dallas. So there it was, a footnote to history. But sometimes footnotes can shed light on dark shadows, and that is precisely what happened in the case of "Jim Braden."

II

FACT OR FICTION

In January of 1969, shortly before District Attorney Jim Garrison was to begin prosecuting his ill-fated JFK conspiracy trial in New Orleans, I met in Los Angeles with a man who had been associated with the Garrison investigation, a former FBI agent named William W. Turner. Turner became a prolific author and one of J. Edgar Hoover's severest critics upon leaving the bureau.

Because I was a producer with CBS Television, Turner wanted me to broadcast the film of the JFK assassination made by amateur photographer Abraham Zapruder, in the apparent belief that it would generate interest in the Garrison investigation—and also give it a degree of credibility. The 8mm film belonged to *Life* magazine, which paid Zapruder an estimated $250,000 for it. (CBS dropped out of the bidding after the price rose above $25,000.)

The authenticity of the film was established by one of the oldest cinema research companies in Hollywood. There were no frames missing as had been widely reported. (What wasn't established was how the former FBI agent had obtained the film, since it was supposed to be locked in a vault at *Life* magazine's office in New York.)

There were compelling elements in the film to indicate that there could have been more than one assassin in Dealey Plaza. The film clearly shows Kennedy being shot from the rear. He clutches his throat and falls forward after the initial rifle burst from the Texas Book Depository. Then suddenly there appears to be another rifle burst from a forward position. The President lurches violently backward, crashing into the rear seat of his limousine, then finally falling to his left against the side of his wife, Jacqueline. I first viewed the film in the presence of the man who was Chief Deputy Attorney General of California at that time, Charles O'Brien. It virtually convinced O'Brien that there was more than one gunman in Dealey Plaza. O'Brien suggested that one would have to ignore the law of physics to explain that violent lurch backward by the President if the only shots fired at him came from the Texas Book Depository, to the rear.

I tried to broadcast the Zapruder film over KNXT, the CBS Television outlet in Los Angeles, but was stopped by *Life* magazine, which claimed sole distribution rights and warned me of the possibility of legal action. *Life* had never shown the film to a public audience for reasons that have never been explained. I was disillusioned to learn that the lawyer retained by CBS to investigate the possibility of running the Zapruder film was also on the payroll of *Life*. And it was he who made it crystal clear that we could not broadcast the film.

Bill Turner was also disillusioned by the inability of the Columbia Broadcasting System to, in his words, "bring the truth to the public." During our conversations I had expressed my doubts about the Garrison investigation in New Orleans. And despite what I had seen on the Zapruder film and my tremendous desire to show it on television, I had strong reservations about becoming an unwitting tool in the Garrison investigation and prosecution.

In parting, the former FBI man told me he shared my reservations about Garrison to some extent but said someone had to bring the truth out into the open. Turner also suggested that I check on a man named Jim Braden, who was believed to be living somewhere in southern California, perhaps in Los Angeles. He said that as best he could determine, Braden was a mystery man in the sequence of events at Dealey Plaza. He had been arrested and released, and then had left Dallas, moved to California, and apparently changed his name. That wasn't really too much to go on, but it made me slightly curious. One thing that particularly interested me was that Oswald, while serving in the Marine Corps, had been stationed near Los Angeles. Furthermore, intelligence agencies in California had picked up rumbles over the years to the effect that Oswald was connected with paramilitary, right-wing organizations. It appeared to be a longshot, but I set out in search of Jim Braden. After searching through nineteen volumes of the Warren Report (the indexing leaves much to be desired) I found the entry concerning his being taken into custody in the Decker Exhibit. There still wasn't much to go on. Braden no longer lived at the address given in the Warren Report, 621 S. Barrington Drive, which is in suburban Westwood near the campus of the University of California at Los Angeles. And he no longer worked at the address listed in the Warren Report, 215 South La Cienega Boulevard, Beverly Hills. There was no indication that he was anywhere in the Los Angeles metropolitan area.

The only thing I had to go on was Braden's driver's license, which Deputy Lummie Lewis had jotted down as "H751755." (The "H" indicated the license had been issued in California in the early 1950s.) The next step was to check with the California Department of Motor Vehicles at its headquarters in the capitol at Sacramento. I was advised that license H751755 belonged to one Jim Braden, and that he had renewed it in the city of Oceanside, in San Diego County, in November of 1966. The department's records showed that Braden lived in the community of Lake San Marcos, not far from Oceanside, but for business reasons preferred to use the address of 380 South Beverly Drive, Beverly Hills, which was a distance of about one hundred miles from his home. Was there anything else I should know about Mr.

Braden? Yes there was, the department advised me. Originally, the license had been issued to him under the name of Eugene Hale Brading, but on September 10, 1963, a little more than two months before the assassination in Dallas, Brading notified the Department he had changed his name to Jim Braden and requested a new license bearing that identification. The new license was promptly issued, and Brading was carrying it when he was taken into custody in Dealey Plaza on November 22, 1963. Next step: try and find out something about the "new" person I had discovered, Eugene Hale Brading.

A call to the California Attorney General's Intelligence Division in Sacramento was greeted with incredulity. "What's this guy done now?" the voice on the end of the line wanted to know. I was reluctant to say, for in fact I didn't know, and my source finally came through with an answer of sorts. "Brading," he said, "is a real bad guy. He's got a long rap sheet and apparently has Mafia connections." I asked for the rap sheet—the summary of an individual's arrests—but it was denied me. Apparently it was just too hot for me to handle. I knew it was worthless to try the FBI, so I contacted a friend of mine, a sheriff in a small county in Texas. It is pretty much routine for a sheriff to obtain an arrest record provided he doesn't give the FBI too many problems. And in this case I was lucky.

Eugene Hale Brading's rap sheet almost blew my mind. There were thirty-five different entries, covering a wide range of activities. Among them were operating a gambling house in Miami, car theft, receiving stolen property, selling World War II gas ration coupons on the black market, mail fraud, embezzlement, and even shoplifting.

Most of the arrests were made under the name of Eugene Hale Brading. However, the FBI dossier showed Brading had used such aliases as Harry Eugene Bradley, James Bradley Lee, Gene Brady, James Lee Cole, and of course Jim Braden, which was the last entry on the rap sheet, having been placed there several months after John Kennedy's assassination. I made this discovery many months after Jim Garrison had announced in New Orleans that a grand jury in that city had accused one Edgar Eugene Bradley, of North Hollywood, California, of taking part in the conspiracy to murder the President of the United States.

I was struck by the similarity between the two names. Both men were known as Gene—Gene Brading, Gene Bradley. Brading had an extensive criminal record; Bradley had none. Brading was in Dealey Plaza the day of John Kennedy's assassination; Bradley was also in Texas that same day but apparently in a city far removed from the scene of the crime. "Why," I asked myself, "had Jim Garrison singled out Gene Bradley to charge with complicity in the assassination but never made any mention of Gene Brading?

There was another interesting fact about Brading in the FBI rap sheet. A flash notation—the last entry in his file—said that if Brading were arrested prior to December 19, 1965, the United States Board of Parole should be notified. Perhaps, I conceded, that was a reasonable explanation for his not revealing his true identity in Dallas the day of the assassination. But then again, perhaps it wasn't. In any event, I considered Gene Brading worthy of further investigation.

At this point I decided on two courses of action. Los Angeles police were in the middle of their investigation of the slaying of Senator Robert Kennedy, which had taken place on June 6, 1968, so first I decided to tell them what I knew. I informed LAPD Chief of Detectives, Rogert Houghton, of the mix-up in Dealey Plaza, and the fact that Jim Braden was, in reality, Eugene Hale Brading. After a cursory examination of his own intelligence files, which revealed Brading had been associated with organized crime for many years, Houghton ordered an immediate investigation. He quickly determined that Brading had been in Los Angeles the night Robert Kennedy was murdered, and we both wondered how many men had been present in both Dallas and Los Angeles for both assassinations.

The second course of action was to present the information to a friend of long standing and a former classmate, the United States Attorney for Southern California, William Matthew "Matt" Byrne, Jr. Byrne was the son of a federal judge, had been appointed to the federal bench by President Johnson. But Byrne was a liberal Democrat, and Republican Senator George Murphy flexed enough political muscle to kill the nomination.

However, President Nixon and then United States Attorney General John Mitchell had a great deal of respect for Byrne's ability as a lawyer, and he was given a Presidential appointment as Executive Director of the Federal Commission on Campus Unrest, headed by William Scranton, a former governor of Pennsylvania, and set up in the wake of the slaughter of students by National Guardsmen during the rioting at Kent State University. The Commission's findings did not exactly endear Byrne and Scranton to certain persons at the White House, particularly Vice-President Spiro Agnew, since it charged that inaction at all levels of government had contributed to the violence at Kent State and at other campuses across the country.

Nevertheless, after Matt Byrne concluded his duties with the Commission, Mr. Nixon reappointed him to the United States District Court in Southern California, and this time there was no opposition from the United States Senate, since Republican George Murphy had lost his seat to Democrat John Tunney.

It was Judge Byrne's misfortune to be chosen to preside at the Pentagon Papers trial in his first major assignment on the Federal bench, and thus become an unwitting participant in one of the most sordid legal affairs of the Twentieth century. The defendants, Dr. Daniel Ellsberg and Anthony

Russo, had been charged with conspiracy, theft, and espionage because they had leaked a top-secret Defense Department study of the Vietnam War to the news media. It became a matter of public record that during the trial White House aides proposed that Byrne replace the late J. Edgar Hoover as head of the FBI, an offer that most observers considered a form of enticement to make certain that Ellsberg and Russo were convicted. But Judge Byrne ignored the offer, and finally threw out the entire case following an admission by the United States Justice Department that the so-called White House plumbers, led by the convicted Watergate bugger, E. Howard Hunt, had burglarized the office of Daniel Ellsberg's psychiatrist in Beverly Hills. That, of course, was the measure of the man who was—in my opinion —beholden to no one, and that is why I contacted him in 1969 when he was still United States Attorney for Southern California, confident that he would help me unravel the mystery of Jim Braden in Dealey Plaza. I had known Byrne for many years, and I simply called and told him that I would like an appointment to discuss the Kennedy assassination. I went with fellow CBS newsman Jack Fox to Byrne's office in the United States Courthouse in downtown Los Angeles. Byrne had invited two others to the meeting—his chief deputy, Robert Brosio, and an FBI agent who was assigned to investigate the assassination of Senator Robert Kennedy.

It was quickly apparent that Byrne, Brosio, and

the FBI agent thought I wanted to talk about RFK's death. "No," I said. "The man I want to discuss with you is named Jim Braden."

The FBI agent had a knowing expression on his face, and he immediately interrupted me. "You mean," he said, "that oil man who works in Beverly Hills?"

"Yes," I responded.

"Yeah, we interviewed him after John Kennedy was murdered," the agent said. "Two guys from our office went out and talked to him."

I then laid the story on the line. Jim Braden was really Eugene Hale Brading, ex-convict; a man linked over the years to the Mafia. The FBI agent refused to believe my story, shaking his head. Byrne was receptive and took notes, but his assistant, Brosio, joined with the FBI agent in the head-shaking. "Even, if what you say is true," Bronsio told me, "it's just another coincidence. The world is filled with coincidences." I felt foolish at times during the conversation, but Byrne kept soliciting information from me. He wanted to make sure I had notified the Los Angeles police of Brading's presence in the city. I assured him I had already talked to Bob Houghton, LAPD Chief of Detectives. "Good," he said, "I'll be expecting a report from him."

As the meeting broke up, the FBI agent seemed incredulous about what I had said. After all, the American public and the FBI itself are conditioned to believe that J. Edgar Hoover's troops always get their man. I honestly expected the matter to

33

die in the United States Attorney's office, because I was not overwhelmed by the response of the others present.

But the next day the FBI agent called me and said, "Pete, if you'll read me the first three numbers on Eugene Hale Brading's rap sheet I'll read you the last three and we can decide if we're talking about the same man." So, thinking it a slightly silly game, I said, "799."

The agent shot back: "431."

"Well," I said, slightly proud of myself, "that means we're talking about the same man, since the last entry on the rap sheet is that of Jim Braden." The agent, sounding as if he had a lump in his throat, suggested we get together shortly.

At the meeting that followed, the agent openly acknowledged that someone had made a mistake, that the FBI had not known until I told Byrne and the others at the meeting that Eugene Hale Brading and Jim Braden were one and the same person.

During the course of that conversation, the FBI agent and I discovered we had both dug up some interesting background information about Eugene Hale Brading. He was headquartered at the notorious La Costa Country Club, in San Diego County, about twenty miles south of President Nixon's Western White House at San Clemente. To intelligence officers in Southern California, La Costa is considered a monument to organized crime, a Mafia watering hole that some policemen have dubbed "Apalachin West." The La Costa

34

development was financed by a multimillion dollar loan from James Riddle Hoffa's Teamsters Union pension fund. At any given moment a major figure in the organized underworld could be found bellying up to the bar at La Costa, more often than not within earshot of a prominent politician. (During the United States Senate's Watergate hearings ex-counsel to the White House, John Dean, testified that he attended a meeting at La Costa, where he and others involved in the scandal discussed the abortive cover-up.)

The fact that Eugene Hale Brading was a "regular" at La Costa was disturbing to the FBI. But perhaps more disturbing was what occurred one week before I revealed Jim Braden's true identity in Matt Byrne's office. It happened that another FBI agent from the bureau's office in Oceanside had questioned Braden at La Costa, believing *Braden* to be his real name and totally unaware that he was an ex-convict whose career in organized crime dated back many years. Ironically, the subject of that conversation with Brading concerned organized crime and a gambling operation with its roots in Dallas, Texas.

While readily admitting that someone had made a mistake in not checking out "Jim Braden" fully in both Dallas and Los Angeles following the JFK assassination, the FBI agent I had first met in Matt Byrne's office implied that the President's murder and the investigation—which was actually the responsibility of the bureau's Dallas office—should be considered ancient history.

The agent then suggested that I might do well to fictionalize what I had uncovered. "It would make a damn interesting story."

There may have been a certain amount of wisdom in what he said, considering the countless difficulties I had in getting this book published. But all things considered, I was a working newsman and fiction just wasn't my bag.

III

A PROFILE OF GENE BRADING

Robert Houghton, Chief of Detectives of the Los Angeles Police Department, eventually satisfied himself after several thousand man-hours of investigation that Eugene Hale Brading was not connected with the assassination of Senator Robert Kennedy. Shortly after Houghton began working the RFK case, he signed a contract with Random House to write a book about the assassination called "Special Unit Senator." That was the name Houghton had given his investigating task force looking into Robert Kennedy's murder. In the police department, the task force was better known as the SUS detail.

In his book Houghton never mentioned Brading by name, but did refer to him on the basis of the information I had provided.

Of Brading and the JFK assassination, Houghton wrote, "The man they discovered was in Dallas on that black day and was apprehended in a building opposite the now famous Texas Book Depository. In addition to his Mafia and oil contacts, he was friendly with 'far right' industrialists and political leaders of that area. . . ."

No one bothered to press Bob Houghton for additional details, but there it was in black and white for the public record: a man associated with the Mafia and right-wing extremists (two groups not necessarily mutually exclusive) was at the scene of the JFK assassination under circumstances never revealed to the American public, much less explained to them.

The SUS task force compiled a comprehensive report on Gene Brading, then turned it over to the FBI. The investigators who made the report stressed to me that they regarded it as a matter of great importance and fully anticipated it would be turned over to United States Attorney Matt Byrne. Their paramount interest, or so they told me, was in the possible role organized crime might have played in the JFK assassination. By coincidence, at that time Matt Byrne's office was conducting an extensive investigation of the Mafia. And I was quite interested in Byrne's decision to subpoena one of the most powerful figures in the Cosa Nostra, the tough and vicious Carlos Marcello, of New Orleans, who had made no secret of his contempt and hatred for both John and Robert Kennedy.

But Byrne always insisted to me that he was never given the SUS report on Brading by the FBI, which under the late J. Edgar Hoover had an announced policy of giving United States Attorneys only such information as the bureau deemed necessary for prosecution.

Despite the official roadblocks set up by the FBI there was a great body of information available. Material I obtained personally from members of the SUS task force, the United States Probation Department, the California Attorney General, and newspaper morgues demonstrated how Gene Brading rose from petty thief to a ranking member of the underworld with the connections Robert Houghton described in his book: the Mafia, oil men, and "far right" industrialists.

Eugene Hale Brading was one of three sons born to Charles and Millie Brading, a relatively poor but hard-working couple from the plains of Kansas. It was a closely knit family, and many years later, when Brading acquired a degree of affluence, he purchased a retirement home for his parents in the coastal city of Santa Barbara, California.

Gene Brading was only nineteen when he was first sentenced to prison in Kansas for burglary in 1934. In the opinion of a parole officer, who knew him well, the sentence was much worse than the crime. The parole officer believed it had been a mistake to confine a youth such as Brading with hardened criminals, who could have an influence in shaping his outlook on life.

Brading was paroled from the Kansas prison in 1938, and proceeded to move to a much faster-paced environment in Miami, Florida, where he quickly became associated with the hoodlum element. On February 24, 1941, he was arrested in Miami for running a gambling house. He was fined $200 after being convicted of bookmaking, and was given a suspended six-month jail sentence. On three different occasions he was arrested in Florida for selling World War II gasoline-ration coupons on the black market. The third time he was sentenced to one year in jail.

Intelligence information indicated that Brading was slowly weaving his way into the mob's hierarchy and that he was a man who was going places. In 1948 while using the alias of Harry Eugene Bradley, he was arrested in Camden, New Jersey, as a material witness in a criminal case. (Camden police have since refused to divulge any details concerning that arrest, but it must be noted that there was considerable organized crime in the Camden area at the time, and Brading's sudden appearance there came as no surprise to investigators who have studied his background.)

Sometime in 1950 Brading moved to El Paso, Texas, and became associated with Victor Emmanuel Pereira, a self-described sportsman and confidant of the Mafia's ranking echelons. Their friendship turned out to be a profitable one.

Brading and Pereira embarked on the country-club circuit, searching for wealthy widows. Both were sharp dressers, good conversationalists, and gave the impression that they were well-to-do. Among their initial acquaintances was a Mrs. Gertrude Joyce, a rich widow from Roswell, New Mexico. She was fair game for the two con men traveling in tandem, and shortly after her first blush of romance with Pereira, he proposed and she accepted. The bride was approximately fifteen years older than the groom, but that didn't dim the enthusiasm as far as Pereira and Brading were concerned, because Mrs. Joyce's bank account was bulging.

Shortly after the nuptials, Brading and Pereira vanished, and the spurned wife became incensed and told her story to law-enforcement officers.

On August 11, 1951, FBI agents arrested Brading and Pereira in New York City on a fugitive warrant issued in Texas that accused them of embezzling $50,000 from Mrs. Joyce. According to the FBI, at the time of their arrest Brading and Pereira were setting their sights on even bigger game aboard a ship in New York harbor, where they were trying to woo the young daughter of a multimillionaire as she was about to set sail for Argentina with her father.

The FBI gave this official account of how Brading and Pereira swindled Mrs. Joyce:

Pereira and Brading met Mrs. Joyce and her sister at a hotel in El Paso, Texas, on April 19, 1951, with Pereira posing as a wealthy sportsman and Brading as an oil land operator. They began paying court to the women and were invited to Mrs. Joyce's home in Roswell, New Mexico. Pereira married Mrs. Joyce in Kansas City, Missouri, following a cross-country trip, on May 25, and Brading became engaged to her sister.

Pereira obtained $5,000 from Mrs. Joyce by telling her he needed the money for a business deal and was temporarily without ready funds. Shortly after the wedding Mrs. Joyce also gave Pereira a $6,900 convertible automobile. Later Pereira and Brading told Mrs. Joyce they had an option to buy the Washington Hotel in Greenville, Texas, for 'a song' and needed $35,286.78 to effect the deal. She gave them the money by check. They cashed it on an El Paso bank, then fled.

Subsequent investigation revealed that Pereira had previously been married three or four times and that he used the $6,900 convertible to pacify the wrath of one of his former wives, who apparently was upset over her failure to receive alimony payments. Once back in custody in Texas, Pereira and Brading maintained that they had lost all of Mrs. Joyce's money on the gambling tables at Juárez, Mexico.

The Texas press instinctively dubbed Brading and Pereira the "love bird swindlers." As the newspapers put it, "They made love, then flew the coop." At the time, the story of their swindle was considered a somewhat sensational news event in the Texas press.

Mrs. Joyce explained that she had become smitten with Pereira because "he was so attractive, and he was heartbroken over a previous divorce. He said he was alone in the world and very lonely."

Brading and Pereira went on trial in United States District Court in El Paso on September 4, 1951, and were quickly found guilty on charges of transporting a check obtained by fraud on interstate commerce, conspiracy to defraud, and using the mails to defraud. Each was sentenced to a dozen years in prison, but the court permitted them to remain free on bail while they appealed their convictions.

Meanwhile the "love birds" were confronted with several serious financial problems. Mrs. Joyce had sued Pereira to get back the money she had loaned him and had received a favorable verdict in the court of United States District Judge Sarah Hughes (the same jurist who administered the Presidential oath to Lyndon Johnson at Love Field, in Dallas, following the JFK assassination).

To compound the financial dilemma, there was word from Austin, Texas, that the Bureau of Internal Revenue had filed a tax lien against Brading for $122,364 and another against Pereira for $22,364. Texas newspapermen expressed more than the usual curiosity about the tax lien against Brading, because it indicated he had had an enormous income over the years.

There was a suspicion that Brading might have connections with organized crime. However, James Connor, chief of intelligence for the Internal Revenue Service in Austin, said he could not legally disclose the sources of Brading's income.

At this point the "love birds" were front-page items throughout Texas, but that did not disturb them one iota. Confronted with a financial headache, they showed amazing dexterity in finding a quick solution to their economic woes. In this case, the solution was another lonely widow, Mrs. D. A. Little, whose late husband had been president of the Magnolia Oil Company from 1933 until failing health forced him to resign in 1945. (Magnolia Oil was one of the giants of the oil industry in Texas until it merged with Socony-Mobil.) Little was a multimillionaire when he died, and his widow was handsomely endowed.

The "love birds" resolved their financial problems when, on August 7, 1952, Pereira and Mrs. Little were married in Cheyenne, Wyoming. Gene Brading was the best man. The newlyweds and the best man moved into the mansion bequeathed by D. A. Little, on Turtle Creek Drive, in the exclusive Dallas suburb of University Park. (Eleven years later the man known as Jim Braden would tell FBI agents in Los Angeles that he was not familiar with Dallas.)

Several months before the marriage in Wyoming, Forrest Keene, Police Chief of University Park, called on Mrs. Little and advised her that Pereira had a most unusual criminal background and that he specialized in bilking rich widows. He suggested that Mrs. Little look elsewhere for male companionship. The Chief said Mrs. Little

44

rebuffed him in no uncertain terms, "telling me to mind my own business.'

When the newlyweds returned to University Park, with Gene Brading playing the third-man theme, Chief Keene decided he had had enough. Pereira specialized in rich widows; Brading specialized in everything. Two weeks after the wedding, Keen sent word that he would like Brading to pay him a visit at the University Park police station. Brading promptly checked in at the station for a tête-à-tête with the Chief that ended almost before it began. Chief Keene arrested Brading for vagrancy, explaining, "He's been hanging around town doing no work that we know of." Gene Brading insisted that he was staying with friends and that he was a legitimate businessman actively involved in the oil industry. But his pleas fell on deaf ears; Chief Keene ordered him locked up.

Then, according to a story published in the *Dallas Morning News* on August 21, 1952, Victor Pereira came to the rescue, paying Brading's $50 fine for vagrancy at the University Park police station. However, in the interim Brading had been transferred to a cell at the Sheriff's headquarters in Dallas. Police Chief Keene instructed authorities at the county jail that Brading's fine had been paid and he could be released. But Bill Decker, the Sheriff of Dallas County, didn't quite see it that way.

When Pereira arrived in his Cadillac at the jail to pick up Brading, the reception wasn't exactly flattering. Sheriff Decker ordered Pereira "mugged and fingerprinted on general principles."

After a long delay, Sheriff Decker finally decided to release both Brading and Pereira on the proviso that Brading get out of Dallas County within forty-eight hours. Brading asked why he was being harassed, and Decker angrily responded, "You're in my county now. That's the reason, if you want to know."

While walking out of the jail, Brading charged that he and Pereira were being "persecuted" by Dallas authorities. The *Dallas Morning News* quoted Brading as saying: "They have mug shots and fingerprints of us all over the country. They've been treating us like this for over a year now."

Despite his displeasure, Brading complied with the deadline for leaving Dallas. Taking part in the evacuation with him were Victor Pereira, of course, and the former Mrs. D. A. Little. Following the precendent set in Dallas, the trio regrouped under the same roof at their next stop, Denver, Colorado. Brading and Pereira were still free on bail while lawyers appealed their convictions, and there was no running out on the new Mrs. Pereira, since she controlled the purse strings.

In late 1969 I phoned Bill Decker and asked if he was aware that the "Jim Braden" his deputies had taken into custody the day of the JFK assassination was really Eugene Hale Brading.

There was at least a minute of silence. Then, Decker gasped, "My God, I remember that guy. He was one of those fast-talking operators who worked on rich widows." I told Decker I was well aware of that, but did he know that Deputy Lummie Lewis actually had Brading in custody on November 22, 1963? Decker never gave a direct answer to that question. He mumbled something about how he'd once run Brading out of town and promised to get back to me for further discussion. "You know," Decker said in closing, "that guy still has a lot of connections down this way."

Bill Decker never did pursue the matter further with me. He died a few months after we had talked.

Once ensconced in Denver, Brading and Pereira associated themselves with the two leading Mafia figures in the Rockies, the brothers Eugene and Clyde Smaldone, also known as Checkers and Flip Flop. Intelligence officers in Colorado were quick to note the association. Brading and Pereira were both extremely clever, and seemed to have a way with money, as well as a ready source of it in the former Mrs. Little. The Smaldones were rough-and-tumble members of the Brotherhood, with a minimum of finesse and a maximum of muscle. At one time Checkers and Flip Flop were credited with controlling the entire city of Pueblo and also the lucrative vending-machine market that stretched from the Rockies to Chicago.

Information gathered by Mafia watchers indicated that Brading and Pereira were strictly big league, that they were actively involved in many transactions with the Smaldone brothers and were regarded as close personal associates. (A few years later, when Gene Brading was imprisoned on the Texas swindling conviction, federal prison authorities took note of the fact that the Smaldones wrote him letters, seeking his advice on business matters.)

During their days in Denver, Brading and Pereira frequently traveled to California, and eventually both moved to Beverly Hills, a favorite nesting spot for underworld figures with some stature. It wasn't too long before their activities attracted the attention of the Mafia-watchers in the Los Angeles Police Department's intelligence unit.

Of particular interest to the detectives whose beat is organized crime was a relationship Brading and Pereira had formed with two newly arrived "oil speculators" from Miami, Arthur Lewis Clark, Sr., and Roger Bauman. Clark generated more than idle curiosity, since he was one of the leaders of the old Purple Gang that operated out of Youngstown, Ohio, and Detroit, Michigan. LAPD intelligence stuck a tail on Clark and Bauman, secretly photographing them with hidden cameras, and establishing a long file on their underworld associates. One of those associates was Eugene Hale Brading.

In 1956 one of the foremost Mafia-fighters in the United States, LAPD's late Chief of Intelligence, Captain James Hamilton, wrote a letter to the Crime Commission of Greater Miami seeking information about Clark and Bauman. Here is part of Hamilton's letter:

> This Department has under investigation Arthur Lewis Clark, Sr., FBI 3709258, and a Roger Bauman. These men are representing themselves as officials of the Sunbeam Oil Company, 212 Roosevelt Theater Building, Miami Beach, and both are spending money very lavishly.
>
> Clark has been arrested several times and has been associated with many confidence men and hoodlums such as James Fratianno, Victor Pereira, Eugene Brading, Clarence Rhodes, Stephen Sambor and the Smaldone brothers of Denver.

That was in 1956! The men lumped together with Brading consisted of a *Who's Who* of organized crime from the Rockies to California.

For the record, Daniel P. Sullivan, Operating Director of the Crime Commission of Greater Miami, did respond to Hamilton. He described Clark and Bauman's oil operation as follows:

> The Sunbeam Oil Company has offices in Miami Beach. It appears to me that this is a pure "front" for con men schemes. The Sunbeam Oil Company is not listed in current directories.

At the time the correspondence was exchanged between the LAPD and the Crime Commission in Miami, little was known about Clark's sidekick, Roger Bauman, other than the fact that he gave the appearance in public of being a gregarious playboy. Eventually, however, Bauman became moderately successful in the oil industry, and Gene Brading could be frequently found at his side.

These were definitely prime members of the underworld, and there is no implication of guilt by association on the part of Captain James Hamilton, who, before he died, was Chief Investigator for the National Football League at a time when the men who ran the professional game were seriously concerned about Mafia attempts to put the squeeze on players by gaining control of their contracts.

Of all the men singled out in the letter by Captain Hamilton, none was more important in the pecking order of organized crime than James Fratianno, a killer known to his enemies as "Jimmie the Weasel."

The Italian-born Fratianno, who had as many aliases as Gene Brading, could easily have been the inspiration for Luca Brasi, the fictional executioner for Vito Corleone in *The Godfather*.

But Brasi pales in comparison with James Fratianno. In 1959 Captain James Hamilton was asked to testify before the California Legislature's Rackets Committee about the Mafia on the West Coast and Fratianno in particular.

Hamilton didn't waste any time in zeroing in on Fratianno. He told the investigating committee,

"We have long considered Fratianno to be the executioner for the Mafia on the West Coast."

Some of the legislators seemed surprised that the Mafia even existed in California. For many years Hamilton's boss, the late Los Angeles Police Chief William Parker, had publicly denied the existence of organized crime anywhere in his bailiwick.

Asked to be specific, Captain Hamilton told the Rackets Committee that his intelligence officers had linked Fratianno to at least sixteen gangland executions. Later the figure was placed at closer to twenty.

Fratianno achieved nationwide notoriety in 1969 when *Look* magazine fingered him as one of the principals in its exposé of Mayor Joseph Alioto, of San Francisco. At the time Alioto was actively seeking the Democratic nomination for Governor of California. *Look* alleged that Alioto and Fratianno were personal associates; and that during a ten-month period in 1965 the Cosa Nostra killer received a series of loans totalling $105,000 from the First San Francisco Bank through the intercession of Alioto, who was one of the founders of the bank and chairman of the board of Directors.

The mayor admitted that Fratianno was a "casual acquaintance," although he denied using any influence to secure the loans for Jimmy the Weasel. Further, Alioto insisted he was unaware that Fratianno was a member of the Mafia, much less an executioner.

To quote Alioto:

> I have no information as to what State and
> Federal authorities now believe to be true
> about Fratianno. I have no information about
> Fratianno's arrest or conviction record. At the
> time I met him I did not know of his criminal
> record, and had no facts or knowledge which
> would have led to the belief he was an un-
> derworld figure.

If Alioto was indeed unaware that Fratianno
was a Mafia killer, he was one of the most naive
politicians in California. Following the *Look*
story Alioto dropped out of the race for Governor,
and although he was subsequently reelected
mayor of San Francisco, political observers believed that his hopes for statewide or national
office had been destroyed by the admitted association with Fratianno.

In the underworld, people like Gene Brading
supply the brains; the Fratiannos supply the muscle and the gunpowder.

One of the more spectacular crimes to which
Fratianno was linked was the attempted assassination in 1949 of Los Angeles gangland figure Mickey Cohen, a member of the so-called Jewish
Mafia." In that shootout, Neddie Herbert, one of
Cohen's closest associates, was killed. Police arrested Fratianno, his brother Warren, and two
other hoodlums in connection with the plot, but
all were released because of insufficient evidence.

Fratianno had the perfect alibi: he was at the home of Nick Licata the night of the shoot-out, and Licata would swear to it. At that time police intelligence was unaware that Licata was weaving his way to the top of the Mafia's trellis and would eventually take control of the family in Los Angeles. What's more, upon assuming power, Licata would also be given autonomous control over another city in another state—Dallas, Texas. Once more, a curious coincidence.

And it was an even greater coincidence that the Los Angeles Police intelligence unit had lumped Gene Brading and Jimmy Fratianno together in the same circle of underworld acquaintances.

Fratianno was also suspected of complicity in the 1951 murders of the "two Tonys" from Kansas City. Tony Brancato and Tony Trombino had the effrontery to rob the Flamingo Hotel, the Mafia house of pleasure in Las Vegas. Their bodies were found in a car parked near Sunset Strip, their skulls blasted behind the ear in the best tradition of the Mafia.

Fratianno was also linked to the murder of Harry (Hooky) Rothman, another close associate of Mickey Cohen, and to the disappearance of Frank Niccoli, who had the dubious honor of being known as a member of Cohen's "Seven Dwarfs." One night Niccoli phoned Cohen to tell him he was going to Fratianno's house to break bread. Evidently that wasn't the only thing broken at the dinner table. Niccoli vanished and was never seen again.

Information developed by state investigators in northern California also linked Fratianno to the dynamite execution of Thomas A. Keen in the community of Colma on February 5, 1952. Keen, owner of a company that developed tote boards and betting equipment for dog-racing tracks, was blown to fragments when he started his Cadillac.

It was learned from an informant that Keen owed more than $80,000 to a Mafia-controlled bookmaking operation, and when Keen welched on the debt, a contract was signed for his execution. There was no better man for the job than Jimmy the Weasel. Sources close to Fratianno said this cold-blooded killer was actually delighted when Captain Hamilton identified him as "the executioner for the Mafia," although the thought of seeking libel damages never crossed his mind. When underworld figures met, Fratianno liked to introduce himself this way: "You've heard of me. I'm Jimmy Fratianno, executioner for the Mafia."

But Fratianno went into a blind rage when anyone referred to him as "The Weasel."

In 1953, about the same time Gene Brading permanently relocated in California, Fratianno began to step up in class, showing a new-found interest in something Brading always liked to keep an eye on, the oil business. That same year Fratianno was arrested for trying to extort a 2 percent "royalty kickback" from the Terry Drilling Company, in Los Angeles. George Terry, president of the firm, and Carl Riddell, a major stockholder, testified in court that Fratianno had threatened them with the "vengeance of the Mafia" unless they agreed to make him a participant in the business.

Fratianno had finally encountered someone he couldn't intimidate, and as a result he was convicted of extortion and served more than six years in prison before he was paroled in July of 1960.

Like Brading, Fratianno had many connections within Jimmy Hoffa's Teamster's Union; so, following his release from prison, he decided to go into the trucking business, capitalizing himself with the help of three bank loans (which according to *Look* Magazine he secured through the intercession of Mayor Joseph Alioto) and the apparent encouragement of his friends in the Union.

In 1966, after a series of complaints by truck drivers, Fratianno was convicted on sixteen counts of defrauding his employees by paying them substandard wages on a federally-financed highway project in southern California's Imperial Valley. According to information gathered by the California Attorney General, the Mafia, it appeared, was doing business directly with the United States government. Fratianno's closest associate in the trucking endeavor was another graduate of the Detroit Purple Gang, Leo Moceri, who also had a reputation as a Mafia triggerman.

Fratianno went back to prison, this time for conspiracy to commit petty theft and violating the state labor code. The fact that the Imperial

Valley, one of the richest farming areas in the United States, had almost been controlled at one point by organized crime outraged the area's representative in the state legislature. Assemblyman Victor V. Veysey, speaking on the floor of the legislature, angrily denounced Fratianno as a "Mafia fingerman." That was gentle in comparison with Captain James Hamilton's description of Fratianno ten years earlier, in which he singled him out as the Mafia's executioner on the West Coast and accused him of committing at least sixteen murders.

Brading's association with Fratianno was only one of his credentials with organized crime. There are other salient points to be made.

Brading and his sidekick, Victor Pereira, continued their "business" relationship in California, and were involved in numerous schemes together, with Brading normally finding enough spare time to bilk a rich widow every few months. They had a friendship with Harold "Happy" Meltzer, one of the leading organized crime figures in the world. This connection was first noted by the LAPD when Pereira's name was found on Meltzer's Christmas-card list.

According to the United States Senate Rackets Committee, Meltzer was organized crime's kingpin in two areas, narcotics and union racketeering.

Of Meltzer, a United States Senate Rackets Committee, member wrote in 1964:

Meltzer now is reported to operate a large bookmaking and prostitution syndicate in California. A major figure in the organized underworld, he is known to all the important narcotics traffickers throughout the United States. He has also operated in Oklahoma, Texas, Baltimore, Miami, Las Vegas, Boston, and various areas of Canada, Cuba, Hong Kong, Japan, Hawaii, and the Philippines.

Another Mafia connection made by the "love birds" in Los Angeles was with the notorious Sica family: the brothers Joe, Freddie, and George. In 1950, the United States Attorney in Los Angeles accused Joe and Freddie of presiding over the largest narcotics ring in the United States. The night before the case was set to go to trial, the government's star witness died mysteriously. Abe Davidian, a twenty-nine-year-old dope peddler turned informant, was shot to death in his mother's home in Fresno, California. The murder was never solved, and for lack of evidence the Sicas were released by United States District Judge Harry C. Westover.

"You come to the conclusion," said Judge Westover, "that a crime wave is spreading across the United States."

How does someone in law enforcement keep an eye on Brading and Pereira while they are running with people like the Sicas? For one thing, they watch all financial transactions. Intelligence officers noted that Pereira was selling stock to Freddie Sica. Pereira was particularly high on one new issue, Accurate Electric, and sold $4,500 worth of stock to Freddie.

The relationships with such people as Jimmy Fratianno, Happy Meltzer, and the Sicas were profitable ones for Brading and Pereira. Unfortunately, it was not a continuous association, since the circle was frequently broken up by prison sentences. Such was the case with Eugene Hale Brading and Victor Emanuel Pereira. Just when they were making names for themselves in the underworld, the United States Supreme Court stepped into the act. On February 1, 1954, in what is regarded by many lawyers as a landmark decision, the nation's highest tribunal upheld their embezzlement convictions in El Paso, Texas.

The Court ruled unanimously that Pereira had perpetrated a "monumental fraud" on the widow from Roswell, Mrs. Gertrude Joyce, the actual fraud taking place when the couple was married. Pereira's appeal was based on the contention that his prosecutor violated a long-standing rule against a wife taking the witness stand to testify against her husband.

The opinion against Pereira, written by Chief Justice Earl Warren, stated that there could never have been any violation of that rule in the first place because the marriage itself was part and parcel of the fraud.

However, the Court split five to three in upholding Brading's conviction. Dissenting associate Justices Black, Douglas, and Sherman opined that there was no doubt that Brading participated in the swindle of Mrs. Joyce "in the true fashion of the confidence game." But the dissenting jurists said that Brading's part in the fraud should have been punished by the laws of the state of Texas, since there was no evidence that he had violated federal statutes. The minority opinion said, in part: "Brading is clearly an aider and abettor of the scheme to defraud which a state may punish, but is he an aider and abettor of the federal offense of using the mails to defraud and causing the fraudulent check to be carried across state lines?"

But the minority opinion couldn't save Brading, and he, like Pereira, was ordered to surrender to begin serving his prison sentence.

Brading entered the federal prison system on March 1, 1954, and at various times was confined in Baltimore, Atlanta, Leavenworth, and McNeil Island. His genius did not go unnoticed. Prison officials spoke highly of Brading's ability to teach illiterate inmates to read. It upset those same prison officials slightly when Brading received correspondence from his allies in the Mafia, such as the brothers Smaldone. But nevertheless he was regarded as a model prisoner.

On February 13, 1959, after serving almost five years, Brading was paroled from the McNeil Island Prison, in the state of Washington. Once again, it was back to the affluence of Beverly Hills, and soon Victor Pereira would be at his side again. How frequently does a convict leave prison and end up a few days later in a suite of offices in Beverly Hills? Gene Brading did. Connections are the lifeblood of the underworld, and once they are made they continue whether you are in or out of prison.

This was the man who wound up in Dealey Plaza and was taken into custody under an assumed name the day John Kennedy was murdered. Was his appearance there an accident? Or was this associate of some of the most notorious figures in la Cosa Nostra there for different reasons? To answer that question we must analyze what happened to Gene Brading after he left prison.

IV

ON PAROLE

A high-ranking Los Angeles police officer once told me that it was just one of those curious accidents of history that Eugene Hale Brading was taken into custody in Dallas when John Kennedy was murdered and that Brading happened to be in Los Angeles when Robert Kennedy was assassinated. The officer insisted that Brading was a clever but petty con man and advised me that if he were in my shoes he would "never get a hang-up over a guy like that."

But despite such advice I decided to probe deeper into Brading's background. I was convinced that while Brading might be a con man, his abilities were anything but petty.

In 1960, about one year after his release from prison, Brading found another wealthy widow, Mildred "Millie" Bollman, and they were married after the usual whirlwind romance. According to a background check by the police SUS squad, Millie Bollman was worth about $4 million. Police documents described her as an heiress to the Swift Meat Packing Company fortune.

But further checking by investigative reporter Earl Golz of the *Dallas Morning News*, who had long been trying to unravel the mystery of "Jim Braden" in Dealey Plaza, revealed that the police report was not quite accurate. Mildred Bollman's fortune had the taint of union money behind it. She had come to California from McHenry County, Illinois—a favorite mobster hangout in the 1930s and '40s. Her husband, Bernard Bollman, had died at the McHenry County Hospital on July 19, 1958, about seven months before Brading got out of prison. The local authorities attributed Bollman's death to "an accidental gunshot wound." He was fifty-nine years old.

Bernard Bollman had been indicted for labor racketeering in the 1930s and for fifteen years he was Secretary-Treasurer of a powerful Teamsters, Chauffeurs and Builders Union local in McHenry County. Along the way he amassed a fortune, becoming President and owner of the McHenry Chemical Company.

Following her husband's death, Mrs. Mildred Bollman moved to the exclusive Bel Air section of Los Angeles, where she eventually met Brading, who had that special knack for ferreting out rich widows. According to Millie's acquaintances, it was love at first sight when she met Brading.

Eventually they set up housekeeping in the desert resort of Palm Springs, California, in a mansion once owned by singer Bing Crosby and his wife, actress Kathy Grant. To intelligence officers it appeared that Eugene Hale Brading was slowly

breaking off his connections with the organized underworld, although from time to time he would meet with some of his high-rolling associates in the oil industry. Life had improved considerably since those "love bird" days in Dallas. This time Brading had the cushion of Mildred Bollman's immense fortune behind him, and he gave no indication that he would stage a repeated performance and fly the coop. Millie just had too much money, and besides she had even opened a joint bank account with him, a fact that would eventually prove to be Gene Brading's undoing and leave him almost penniless.

During those salad days in Palm Springs Brading could frequently be found at the plush Thunderbird Country Club, where intelligence officers observed that he regularly participated in the all-night games of chance that went on behind the legal shelter of the private club at the desert spa. Millie confided to friends that she knew all about Gene's past and didn't care one iota. She had found true love.

However, Brading cared when any mention of his past was brought up. And he was seized with rage when word circulated through the grapevine at the Thunderbird Country Club that his marriage to Millie was financed by the mob, which had its sights set on her millions.

And there was still a part of Brading's past that he couldn't cast aside: his association with Victor Emanuel Pereira. Pereira was also doing all right. He and his wife, the former Mrs. D.A. Little, the

Texas oil heiress, were now living at the Beverly Wilshire Hotel, in Beverly Hills. Pereira had become West Coast representative for Earl Scheib, whose specialty was cut-rate car painting. The business became so lucrative that it spread to almost every state in the country. Pereira had also formed a partnership with Scheib in the operation of the Santa Maria Sky Ranch, near Ensenada, Mexico. Ultimately, it was that relationship with Scheib that would trip up both Pereira and Brading.

Since Brading and Pereira had handsome financial bases provided by their wealthy wives, they began acquiring property and making investments. In late 1959, only a few months after his release from prison, Pereira purchased a major interest in the Delco Oil Properties Company, in Texas. Brading subsequently bought into the same firm. They also made a sizable investment in the Matador Oil Company, in Matagorda County, Texas.

Branching out, Brading and Pereira also went into business as the World Oil Company, in the office of the Wallace White Investment Company, 215 South La Cienega Boulevard, Beverly Hills. (That was the same address listed on "Jim Braden's" driver's license when he was taken into custody in Dealey Plaza on November 22, 1963.)

Brading also associated himself with the Morgan Brown Oil Company, based in both Beverly Hills and Santa Barbara. According to its portfolio, the company's specialty was exploring for oil in the tidelands off the California coast. But in reality it was swindling the gullible with phony oil stocks.

Brading dutifully reported his business connections, investments, and income to the United States Parole Office in Los Angeles. One of his acquisitions was the Ladoux Well, in Opelousas, Louisiana.

The federal file on Brading showed that he had an average income of around $1,000 a month from that well until he was released from parole in 1965. There was one exception, however. For November of 1963 Brading reported a net income from the well of $7,642.89.

Brading gave the impression that his association with the Morgan Brown Oil Company based at 449 South Beverly Drive, Beverly Hills, was becoming an uncomfortable arrangement. Parole officers in Los Angeles learned that ill feelings had had developed because Brown had gone to Palm Springs and persuaded Millie Bollman's grown son by a previous marriage to give him $5,000 worth of stock in exchange for a mortgaged airplane and other relatively worthless property.

On January 2, 1962, the California Franchise Tax Board permanently revoked the license of the Morgan Brown Oil Company for repeated failure to pay state taxes, and Brading indicated he was through with Brown forever. But such was not to be the case.

Morgan Brown was a fast operator, and it caught up with him. In 1964 a felony warrant was issued for his arrest and he was criminally charged for selling $10,000 worth of stock in nonexistent oil wells to three prominent Santa Barbara residents. On August 10, 1964, a young Los Angeles policeman was almost killed when he tried to serve the warrant on Brown.

Brown was approaching the West Los Angeles home of his estranged wife when he was spotted by the officer. The oil man took away the officer's gun, stripped off his clothes, tied him up, then started shooting at him wildly. Fortunately, the officer wasn't hurt. Brown fled but two hours later was captured by a dozen policemen in nearby Santa Monica after he barricaded himself in a motel room. At his trial Brown pleaded that he was insane, but to no avail. He was sentenced to state prison and served four years before being paroled.

What is significant here is that Gene Brading insisted he was parting company with Morgan Holbert Brown as early as 1962. Yet on November 21, 1963—the day before the JFK assassination—Brown was one of those who accompanied Brading on his "business trip" to Dallas.

After ostensibly dissolving his relationship with Brown, Brading became the West Coast representative for Roger Bauman, the oil man investigated by Los Angeles police in 1956 because of his underworld connections. Bauman had found greener pastures in Dallas, Texas, where he got to know the sons of H. L. (Herman Lafayette) Hunt, the right-wing oil man who ranks among the world's richest men. Bauman's main office was in the Gulf State Building, in Dallas. But he also maintained another office at 8249 Beverly Boulevard, Beverly Hills, and with a helping hand from Gene Brading, directed the operations of the Bauman Drilling Company, in Louisiana.

In addition to that multitude of holdings, Brading also worked on at least one occasion out of an office in Room 1701 of the Père Marquette Building in New Orleans, where he was said to be associated with an oil geologist named Vernon Main, Jr. Right next door there could frequently be found another man with connections leading right to the top of organized crime—David Ferrie. Coincidence seemed to follow Eugene Brading everywhere he went.

The apparent financial success achieved by the old "love birds" wasn't without its complications on the distaff side. In late 1962 a rift of monumental proportions developed between Pereira and his wife, the former Mrs. Little. She ejected Pereira from their suite at the Beverly Wilshire Hotel and told him to seek bed and board elsewhere.

He called on Brading in Palm Springs and confided that he was deeply in debt. His wife had cut off all his sources of income; he had a number of bad checks outstanding and needed financial assistance immediately. Brading came to the rescue and wrote Pereira a check for $40,000. When Millie found out about the check she was furious and gave Gene his walking papers. On October 24, 1963, the marriage was annulled in Superior Court in Indio, California.

Mrs. Bollman's lawyer, Leonard Beck, maintained that Millie had entered into the marriage unaware that Brading had failed to divorce two previous wives.

Gene Brading was broke. Millie had tied up everything they owned. The great majority of the oil investments had been made with Millie's bankroll, and she wasn't letting go of them. So Brading moved back to the Los Angeles area to live in an apartment in Westwood—a far cry from the old Crosby manor in the desert.

But Brading was lucky compared to his friend, Vic Pereira, who really bit the dust. Pereira's wife was still keeping him under surveillance despite his hasty departure from their hotel suite. Back in the chips with that $40,000 endowment from Brading, Pereira joined his friend and business associate Earl Scheib in an outing at the Santa Anita race track in Arcadia, a suburb of Los Angeles. The high-rolling Scheib suddenly decided that when the races were over, he would take his entourage to Hawaii, paying all expenses. Off went Pereira to the islands with Scheib without notifying his parole officer. It was a critical mistake. Somehow Mrs. Pereira found out about it and blew the whistle on Vic. He was sent back to federal prison as a parole violator.

Eugene Hale Brading had a lot to mull over in his Westwood apartment. Parole officers noted that he had been visibly shaken by what had happened to Pereira. Once he and Pereira had been admonished by parole authorities for making trips in tandem to Louisiana without permission. From that moment on, Gene Brading appeared to advise the Parole Office of his every move.

Things had gone from bad to worse for the "love birds." But as far as Gene Brading was concerned, there were still more deals to be made, more widows to be courted. And what about those old connections in organized crime?

V

THE TIME AND THE PLACE

In the fall of 1963 Eugene Hale Brading seemed to have a multitude of interests in Texas and Louisiana. Shortly after changing the identity on his California driver's license to *Jim Braden*, he made plans to go to the Southwest. His parole officer in Los Angeles gave him permission for a trip to Houston on September 15, 1963, for the purpose of discussing business with one D. D. Ford, a "land man" for the Tidewater Oil Company, owned by J. Paul Getty, the billionaire often described as the world's richest man. There is no record of how long Brading stayed in Houston.

But again, we have one of those curious coincidences. According to the Warren Commission, Lee Harvey Oswald was in Houston on September 25, 1963, en route to Mexico City on that much-publicized trip during which he allegedly hoped to make arrangements to go to Cuba. According to the Warren Commission, Oswald made at least one phone call in Houston. Then, on September 26, he boarded Continental Trailways bus number 5133 for Laredo, Texas.

In October of 1963, the same month Brading's marriage to Mildred Bollman was dissolved, he was given permission to make a second trip to Houston to discuss oil speculation with executives of the Tidewater and Gulf oil companies.

On or around October 27 Brading made plans for still another trip to Houston, to be followed by a visit to Louisiana.

In early November of 1963 Brading informed his parole officer that he wanted to return to Texas on business. He gave the impression that he would be traveling by himself.

He was granted permission to leave Los Angeles for Dallas on November 18. According to the plan presented at the Parole Office, Brading would remain in Dallas until November 21. From Dallas he would go to Houston, then on to Opelousas, Louisiana. He was instructed to check in with the Parole Office in Dallas upon his arrival.

But Brading did not follow his "trip ticket" to the letter. Had he done so, he would not have been picked up in Dealey Plaza the day of the assassination. Federal parole records indicate that Brading checked in with Roger Carroll, the Chief Parole Officer in Dallas, around noon on November 21. Following the meeting, Carroll made a report on Brading's visit, then sent copies of it to the United States Board of Parole headquarters in Washington, D. C., and to Brading's parole officer in Los Angeles.

In that report, Carroll wrote: "He [Brading]

advised that he planned to see Lamar Hunt and other oil speculators while here."

There began the contradictions, the curious co-incidences, and a trail that ultimately leads to Jack Ruby. Later on, when Los Angeles police learned that Brading had indeed been in Dallas at the time of John Kennedy's murder, they decided to interrogate him immediately, mainly to determine what he was doing on the night of June 6, 1968, when Senator Robert Kennedy was slain.

Los Angeles Police Homicide Sergeant Chic Guitierrez, who conducted the interview at Brading's home in Lake San Marcos, California, became somewhat uncomfortable when he noticed an FBI agent he recognized waiting outside the house. Nevertheless he proceeded with the interview, without inviting the FBI man to participate.

As Brading told the story to Guitierrez, he was in the Century Plaza Hotel on the west side of Los Angeles the night of the RFK assassination. The Century Plaza is a drive of about fifteen minutes from the Ambassador, where Robert Kennedy was killed. Then the subject turned to Brading's visit to the Hunt Oil Company, in Texas. Brading denied that such a visit ever took place. He maintained that it had been his business associate, Roger Bauman, who met with Hunt and that two other men, Morgan Holbert Brown and Duane Hermin Nowlin, had been with Bauman, who of course had a long string of connections in the underworld. Morgan Holbert Brown also had many underworld connections, growing out of his past friendship with Brading. And Duane Hermin Nowlin was a professional gambler, who, along with his brother, Jimmy, happened to be well acquainted with the Denver branch of the Mafia family of the brothers Smaldone.

Brading told Sergeant Guitierrez that Bauman, Brown, and Nowlin had legitimate business to conduct at the Hunt Oil Company. Brading said he did not want his business associates to know about his criminal past, so while they were visiting at the Hunt Oil Company, he had secretly checked in at the Federal Parole Office in Dallas. It was a difficult story for the LAPD sergeant to swallow. Brading's reputation was well known in the underworld, and his three associates in Dallas on that day certainly knew all about his past.

Brading explained that on the following day, November 22, he was prepared to leave Dallas, but first had to check out with the Parole Office. He said he watched the Presidential motorcade weave past the Federal Parole Building, John Kennedy waving to the people lining the sidewalk. After the motorcade went by, Brading said, he noticed a parole officer, a "Mr. Flowers," who was going into the Federal Building with his secretary.

On that point, Chief Probation Officer Roger Caroll, of Dallas, countered, "We have no 'Mr. Flowers' employed here nor did we in November of 1963."

As for Brading's story about viewing the motor-cade, Roger Carroll wrote:

> Mr. Brading possibly could have obtained glimpses of President Kennedy from this [Federal] building. However, a much *taller* building would block a direct view of the parade route [which in this end of town was on Harwood Street, one block east of the Federal Building].
>
> This office was closed and we walked over to Harwood Street *in order to get a good view* of the President on November 22, 1963.
>
> I have directed our local FBI's attention to your letter of June 25, 1965.

But back to Sergeant Chic Guitierrez of the LAPD and his interview with Gene Brading.

"Why didn't you give your true name at the Dallas Sheriff's station?" Guitierrez asked.

"They didn't ask me," Brading responded. He went on to say that the night after he was released from custody, he caught a plane to Houston for the purpose of conducting more oil business. This was still another coincidence. The notorious David Ferrie, who, the evidence strongly suggests, was well acquainted with Lee Harvey Oswald, was also en route to Houston that same night.

In summary, Eugene Hale Brading, an ex-convict on federal parole, arrived in Dallas using new identification. He had told his parole officer in Los Angeles that he would be leaving Dallas on November 21; yet on that day he checked in with the parole officer in Dallas to announce his arrival. According to his trip ticket he was supposed to be in Houston on November 22, when he was picked up in Dealey Plaza.

Brading insisted he did not know Lamar Hunt. Yet it is a matter of public record that he advised Parole Officer Roger Carroll that he was in Dallas to see Lamar Hunt.

Paul Rothermel, a former FBI agent, was chief of security for the Hunt Oil Company, in Dallas. He told me it was his distinct impression that Eugene Hale Brading was at the Hunt Oil Company offices in Dallas the day before the JFK assassination. He said the visitor's log for that day showed that Morgan Brown, Duane Nowlin, Roger Bauman, "and friend" had visited the brothers Lamar and Nelson Bunker Hunt. That "friend," in Rothermel's opinion, was Eugene Hale Brading. However, all this must fall into the category of hearsay, since I never saw the visitor's log of the Hunt Oil Company and have been advised that it no longer exists.

Paul Rothermel, however, left the Hunt Oil Company under a cloud. It was reported that he had gathered extensive information on the JFK assassination, and when he departed, he took all his security files with him. Rothermel subsequently charged the Hunt family with tapping his telephone and harassing him, and he filed a massive suit for damages. Originally, he had been employed by the billionaire industrialist H. L. (Herman Lafayette) Hunt, but according to Rother-mel, it was the Hunt sons who manipulated his dismissal.

H. L. Hunt was once quoted as saying that his longtime friend, Lyndon Johnson, "made some terrible mistakes as President, including the selection of Chief Justice Earl Warren to head the inquiry into President Kennedy's assassination." The senior Hunt was also said to be greatly disturbed at the way his family's name was bandied about in the Warren Commission report.

The Warren Commission maintained that Nelson Bunker Hunt (who prefers to be called Bunker) was one of "three wealthy businessmen" who financed a black-bordered ad in the November 22, 1963, *Dallas Morning News*, "welcoming" John Kennedy to Texas by implying that he was a traitor. The politics of the Hunt family are ultra-conservative, but after his father, Nelson Bunker Hunt is the most vocal. In fact, he was one of the chief contributors to Wallace's 1968 presidential campaign, when Wallace ran against Richard Nixon and Hubert Humphrey. Bunker's vast expenditures touched off an extensive investigation by the Internal Revenue Service, which caused his father a great deal of embarrassment. When H. L. Hunt tried to attend President Nixon's inauguration in 1969, he was hustled away by Secret Service agents. Apparently there was a mistaken belief among Mr. Nixon's supporters that H. L. Hunt, rather than his son, was the one who had bankrolled George Wallace.

The Warren Commission devoted considerable time to exploring connections that Oswald's killer, Jack Ruby, might have had with ultraconservative political movements, particularly those generated by the Hunt family. Among Ruby's possessions Dallas police found two scripts from H. L. Hunt's radio program, "Life Line," which was decidedly right-wing. The Commission satisfied itself that Ruby acquired the scripts a few weeks before the JFK assassination in bags of "H.L.H." food items he had picked up at the Texas Products Show. (H.L.H. is a division of the Hunt Oil Company.) The Warren Commission stated:

Ruby is reported to have become enraged when he discovered the scripts, and threatened to send one to "Kennedy." He is not known to have done anything with them prior to giving one to a radio announcer on November 23; and on that day he seemed to confuse organizations of the extreme right with those of the far left.

This was the same Jack Ruby who told Earl Warren that if the truth were to be known, he would have to be taken to a safer place, preferably Washington, D.C.

The FBI also reported that Lamar Hunt's telephone number appeared "in a book which was the property of Jack Ruby." Lamar Hunt, H. L.'s other son, was questioned about that by FBI agent

Lansing P. Logan in Dallas on December 17, 1963. In his report, Logan wrote:

> Mr. Hunt advised that he could not think of any reason why his name would appear in Jack Ruby's personal property and that he had no contact whatsoever with Ruby to the best of his knowledge.

There was one more exhibit in the Warren Report that linked Jack Ruby to the Hunt family: the time and place (November 21, 1963, and the Hunt Oil Company, in Dallas). Both factors, of course, coincide with Gene Brading's alleged movements in Dallas.

The Warren Commission determined that on the day before President Kennedy's assassination, Ruby had driven a young woman to the oil company to see Lamar Hunt. Connie Trammell, an attractive college coed, had become acquainted with Ruby while she was a journalism student at the University of Texas. Miss Trammell first met Ruby at his Carousel Club, where she turned down his offer of a job as a stripper. She said that what she really wanted was a job in public relations.

Miss Trammell told the FBI that she, not Ruby, initiated a job interview with Lamar Hunt at his office. She said that on November 21, 1963, Ruby came to her apartment. According to the Warren Commission, "... they again discussed possible leads for her to secure employment, and he [Ruby] drove her down to the office of Lamar Hunt ...

seemingly to establish a business connection. . . ."
There is no additional elaboration in the Warren
report. The only thing really confirmed was that
Ruby went to the Hunt Oil Company building.
The former FBI agent, Paul Rothermel, said
it was his opinion that Jack Ruby did not go inside
Lamar Hunt's office, unlike Gene Brading, who,
he was convinced, was there.

Ruby's Mafia connections were fairly well
known in intelligence circles, dating back to his
racket days in Chicago. In Dallas he was best described as a tinhorn strip-joint operator who
played it close to the vest with both the police
and the underworld.

Was the fact that Lamar Hunt's name was mentioned in connection with both Jack Ruby and
Gene Brading just another curious coincidence?

As mentioned previously, Eugene Hale Brading
maintained that he flew out of Dallas the night
of the assassination and that his destination was
Houston, Texas. But federal parole records in
Houston do not place him there until four days
later. That would be on November 26, 1963, when
Brading paid a visit to Lawrence E. Miggens,
Chief United States parole officer for the Houston
area.

Miggens filed a report on the visit, and following the usual procedure he sent copies to the parole offices in Washington, D. C., and Los Angeles.

Miggen's report on his meeting with Brading
said in part: "I would like to say that I am impressed with his demeanor and cooperation."

Miggens said it was his opinion that it should be unnecessary for Brading to make any more visits to the United States Parole Office should he have future business dealings in Houston.

I contacted Miggens and told him what I knew about Brading's presence in Dealey Plaza on November 22, 1963, including the fact that he had been taken into custody under the assumed name of Jim Braden.

Here is his response:

LAWRENCE E. MIGGINS
CHIEF PROBATION OFFICER

P. O. BOX 61207
HOUSTON, TEXAS 77061
TEL. CA 8-0611
EXT. 4247

UNITED STATES DISTRICT COURT

OFFICE OF PROBATION OFFICER
SOUTHERN DISTRICT OF TEXAS

August 2, 1969

Mr. Peter Noyes
Managing Editor
KNXT, Channel 2
6121 Sunset Boulevard
Los Angeles, California 90028

Re: Eugene Hale Brading

Dear Mr. Noyes:

Upon receipt of your letter of July 30th, I checked through our old correspondence on the Eugene H. Brading case and I am afraid I have very little to offer you to assist in this rather unusual investigation.

As you probably know from Mr. McEachen's file, Brading was given permission to come to Houston with Parole Board approval September 15, 1963, five days, to discuss alleged business with Mr. D. D. Ford, landman for the Tidewater Oil Company here. He did arrive in Houston, but I am not sure he contacted Mr. Ford because Mr. Brading wrote me a note on Sheraton Lincoln Hotel stationary which was placed under our front door September 16, 1963, at 6:15 PM saying that he was bailing out of Houston early due to the storm and by the time I would receive the note he would be back in Los Angeles.

You probably know that on November 20, 1963, he was given permission to fly to Dallas on business for five days and then it was projected that he was going to Houston on the 25th of November until the 26th when he was expected in Opelousas, Louisiana, before returning to Los Angeles. We have confirmation that he reported to Mr. Roger C. Carroll November 25th at noontime where he expected to remain several days working on an oil deal. He advised Mr. Carroll he planned to see Lamar Hunt and other speculators while there. On November 26th he came to my office at 1:45 PM after he had consulted with officers of the Tidewater Oil Company and he allegedly left that afternoon on his return trip to Los Angeles. He told me he would be seeing USPO Samuel Barrett of the Los Angeles office on the morning of November 27th.

You are quite right in that Mr. Brading did not inform me that he was arrested by the Dallas Sheriff's Office on November 22, 1963, under the name of Jim Braden; however, this is just one of many loose ends left by the Warren Commission.

I presume Mr. Brading stayed at the Sheraton Lincoln Hotel if he remained overnight in Houston on November 25th, but we have no verification as to his exact time of arrival after the assassination.

Sincerely yours,

[*Signature*]

Lawrence E. Miggins, Chief
U. S. Probation Officer

LEM:as

cc: CUSPO Angus D. McEachen
    Los Angeles, California

Parole officer Miggens was obviously correct in observing that Brading's presence in Dealey

Plaza was one of the loose ends left by the Warren Commission.

Perhaps the other loose end, which intrigued me most, was that of the disputed witness in the Warren Commission's investigation—the law-enforcement officer who said he saw what others claimed he couldn't have seen.

VI

THE DISPUTED WITNESS

In 1960 the Dallas County Sheriff's Department honored Deputy Roger Craig as its "Man of the Year" for capturing a dangerous felon. He was considered one of the most promising young men in local law enforcement. But shortly after John Kennedy was murdered, Craig was fired from the Sheriff's Department, his superiors having branded him a "kook." Those superiors conveyed the impression that Roger Craig was chasing shadows on the day of the assassination. For a time Craig went into hiding, after receiving information from one of his few remaining friends in law enforcement that the Mafia had put a price on his head.

It was apparent that Craig had posed questions about the JFK assassination that no one in authority could or would answer. And when Craig insisted on answers to the questions he raised, he lost his job. In the opinion of Warren Commission investigators, Roger Craig was a disputed witness whose testimony contradicted the theory that Lee Harvey Oswald was a solitary killer.

In the panic that followed the assassination, Craig was one of two deputies who almost instinctively set their sights on the Texas Book Depository and its immediate environs. FBI and Secret Service agents appeared somewhat dazed, but Craig and Deputy C. L. "Lummie" Lewis seemed to know precisely what they were doing, and they coordinated their activities in tandem.

It was Deputy Lewis who arrested "Jim Braden" and took him to the Sheriff's station for questioning. Lewis was supicious about "Braden" —but only up to a point. He was not suspicious enough to fingerprint him. Had he done so, he would have quickly discovered that Braden was in reality Eugene Hale Brading, the notorious ex-convict whom Sheriff Bill Decker had run out of Dallas many years before because of his hoodlum activities.

Now, years later, it has been determined that Eugene Hale Brading was in close proximity to the scene of the JFK assassination. Investigator Al Chapman of Dallas spent years gathering photographic evidence of the people in the crowd immediately after the assassination. There was one man wearing a hat and topcoat, his eyes covered by dark glasses, who was isolated in a crowd scene and aroused Chapman's suspicion. He took the photograph to Deputy Lummie Lewis, who quickly identified the man in the picture as the suspect he took into custody on November 22, 1963—the oil man from Beverly Hills, California, Jim Braden.

The Warren Commission apparently never inspected to any great degree the material presented under Deputy Lewis' name in the Decker Exhibit. But the material presented in the same exhibit by Deputy Roger Craig became one of the most controversial matters of the investigation. The Commission ultimately ruled that Craig was not a reliable witness, saying it "could not accept important elements in his testimony."

This is Roger Craig's disputed testimony, his initial report to Sheriff Bill Decker, which ultimately cost him his job as a law-enforcement officer:

I was standing in front of the Sheriff's Office at 505 Main Street, Dallas, Texas, watching President Kennedy pass in the motorcade. I was watching the rest of the motorcade a few seconds after President Kennedy passed where I was standing when I heard a rifle shot and a few seconds later a second and then a third shot. At the retort of the first shot, I started running around the corner and Officer Buddy Walthers and I ran across Houston Street and ran up the terrace on Elm Street and into the railroad yards. We made a round through the railroad yards and I returned to Elm Street by the Turnpike sign at which time Officer Walthers told me that a bullet had struck the curb on the south side of Elm Street. I crossed to Elm with Deputy C. L. Lummie Lewis to search for a spot where a shell might have hit. About this time I heard a shrill whistle and I turned around and saw a white male running down the hill from the direction of the Texas School Book Depository Building and I saw what I think was a light colored Rambler station wagon with luggage rack on top pull over to the curb and the subject who had come running down the hill get into this car. The man driving this station wagon was a dark-complected white male. I tried to get across Elm Street to stop the car and talk with subjects, but the traffic was so heavy I could not make it. I reported this incident at once to a Secret Service Officer, whose name I do not know, then I left this area and went at once to the building and assisted in the search of the building. Later that afternoon I heard that the City had a suspect in custody and I called and reported the information about the suspect running down the hill and getting into a car to Captain [Will] Fritz and was requested to come at once to City Hall. I went to City Hall and identified the subject they had in custody [Oswald] as being the same person I saw running down this hill and get into the station wagon and leave the scene.

One of the critical points made by Craig was that after he had seen Oswald flee from the Book Depository and depart by car, he told a Secret

Service Officer what he had seen. But no one from the Secret Service came forward to verify Craig's story. This would help shatter Craig's credibility with the Warren Commission.

After submitting his report to Sheriff Decker, Craig found himself the object of curiosity in his own department, the Dallas Police, and the FBI. Investigators asked Craig to amplify his original report. Craig explained that he had gone to the Dallas Police interrogation room at City Hall, where Captain Fritz was in the midst of questioning Oswald, a questioning that for some strange reason was never recorded. According to the Warren Commission report, Craig "told Captain Fritz that Oswald was the man he saw. Craig also claimed that Fritz pointed out Oswald to Craig, that Craig . . . identified him. . . . Oswald rose from his chair, looked directly at Fritz, and said, 'Everybody will know who I am now.' "

At first the Warren Commission actually seemed prepared to accept Roger Craig as a credible witness. But then the FBI failed to locate the Secret Service agent whom Craig said he had encountered in Dealey Plaza, and Captain Will Fritz of the Dallas Police Homicide Bureau challenged just about everything Craig told the Warren Commission.

The quote attributed to Oswald by Craig—"Everybody will know who I am now"—was widely publicized and was initially accepted by most observers of the investigation as proof of guilt.

But the Warren Commission apparently felt it had to either accept or reject the entire body of Roger Craig's testimony, because if what the deputy said were true, it would contribute to the theory of a conspiracy.

So the testimony of deputy Roger Craig was rejected out of hand. Of Craig, the Warren Commission wrote:

Captain Fritz stated that a deputy sheriff whom he could not identify did ask to see him that afternoon [November 22, 1963] and told him a similar story to Craig's. Fritz did not bring him [Craig] into his office to identify Oswald but turned him over to a Lieutenant Baker for questioning. If Craig saw Oswald that afternoon, he saw him through the glass windows of the office. And neither Captain Fritz nor any other officer can remember that Oswald dramatically arose from his chair and said, "Everybody will know who I am now." If Oswald had made such a statement, Captain Fritz and the others present would probably have remembered it.

Craig's contention that Oswald escaped from the Texas Book Depository was also at odds with another Commission finding. The Commission concluded, despite tenuous evidence, that after the shooting Oswald calmly walked out of the Book Depository, boarded a bus in the bedlam in

Dealey Plaza and, then, because traffic was so heavy, got off the bus and caught a taxi which took him to his boarding house.

The quickness with which Oswald moved out of Dealey Plaza and finally wound up in the Oak Cliff area of Dallas, where he killed officer J. D. Tippit, has baffled many a critic of the Warren Commission.

Rather than believe the testimony of a deputy Sheriff who swore Oswald made his escape in a car with the help of others, the Commission chose to believe the testimony of an elderly woman, Mary Bledsoe, who had once rented a room to Oswald. Mrs. Bledsoe told the Commission that on November 22 she had gone to Dealey Plaza to watch the Presidential motorcade. She said that after the assassination she boarded a bus at St. Paul and Elm Streets to return home.

Quoting from Mrs. Bledsoe's testimony:

After we got past Akard at Murphy—I figured it out. Let's see. I don't know for sure. Oswald got on. He looks like a maniac. His sleeve was out here. . . . His shirt was undone.

. . . he looked so bad in his face, and his face was so distorted . . . hole in his sleeve right here.

As far as the Warren Commission was concerned, that was sufficient testimony to make Craig a disputed witness. When Oswald was

arrested in a theater shortly after the Tippit killing, he was wearing a brown shirt with a hole in
the elbow. By the time Mrs. Bledsoe was questioned, that information was in the public domain.

Mrs. Bledsoe told the Commission, "As the bus
neared Lamar Street, Oswald left the bus and
disappeared into the crowd."

The bus Oswald was supposed to be aboard was
not headed in the direction of his rooming house,
at 1026 North Beckley. So why would Oswald have
gotten onto it, as Mrs. Bledsoe said? What made
her testimony more valid than that of Deputy
Roger Craig? Mrs. Bledsoe was supposed to have
failing eyesight. Roger Craig was supposed to have
twenty-twenty vision and the credentials of a law-
enforcement officer.

Step two in debunking Craig was the testimony of William Whaley, a forgetful taxicab
driver with a bad sense of direction, who maintained that he picked up Oswald after he got off
the bus. Whaley came forward the day after the
assassination, volunteering that he recognized
Oswald from a newspaper photograph.

To quote Whaley:

You could have picked him [Oswald] out
without identifying him because he was
bawling out the policemen, telling them it
wasn't right to put him in line with these
teenagers and all of that and they asked me

91

which one and I told them. It was him all right, the same man.

He showed no respect for the policemen; he told them what he thought about them. They knew what they were doing and they were trying to railroad him and he wanted his lawyer.

Even the Warren Commission was forced to admit to problems concerning Whaley's testimony. Whaley said Oswald was the second man in the lineup, while in fact, Oswald was the third man. Whaley said there were six men in the lineup with Oswald, but actually there were only four men, only two of them teenagers.

To quote the Commission:

Whaley was somewhat imprecise as to where he unloaded his passenger (Oswald). He marked what he thought was the intersection of Neches and Beckley on a map of Dallas with a large "X." He said, "Yes Sir; that is right because this is the 500 block of North Beckley." However, Neches and Beckley do not intersect. Neches is within one half block of the roominghouse at 1026 North Beckley where Oswald was living. The 500 block of North Beckley is five blocks south of the roominghouse.

Those were just a few of the inconsistencies in Whaley's story; yet ultimately the Warren Commission justified his "eyewitness" account rather than the testimony of Deputy Roger Craig. Whaley was obviously an unreliable witness. He insisted that, when he picked up Oswald, the assassin was wearing a blue jacket, which clashed with the testimony of Mrs. Bledsoe, the witness who placed Oswald aboard the bus. There is no evidence anywhere that Oswald was wearing a jacket after the assassination.

Despite the prodding of Assistant Warren Commission Counsel David W. Bellin, Craig stuck to his original story—the report he signed on November 22, 1963. Captain Will Fritz offered this refutation:

> One deputy sheriff started to talk to me but he was telling me some things that I knew wouldn't help us and I didn't talk to him but somebody else took an affidavit from him. His story that he was telling didn't fit with what we knew to be true.

Assistant Warren Commission Counsel Joseph Ball, a prominent criminal lawyer from Los Angeles, failed to press Captain Fritz further. At that point Ball and his colleagues decided to write off Craig's testimony despite his obvious credentials. Ball, an abrasive man who often defended public officials accused of corruption or other misdeeds, was perhaps the chief architect of the Warren Commission's report on the assassination. Yet Ball, in the interest of expediency, seemed to be willing to take the easy way out by dismissing Roger Craig's story. Over the years Ball had had great experience in dismissing the stories of law-enforcement officers who testified against his clients at criminal trials.

He treated newsmen with the same disdain. When I posed questions to him about the assassination his manner was rude and arrogant. No one had the right to question Joe Ball. But Ball's conclusions notwithstanding, the testimony of Deputy Sheriff Roger Craig is of critical importance in this investigation.

VII

THE ENIGMA IN NEW ORLEANS

Roger Craig testified before the Warren Commission on April 1, 1964. After that he was persona non grata in Dallas. He wandered about somewhat aimlessly until the early part of 1967, when it was disclosed that Jim Garrison, the District Attorney of New Orleans, was conducting his own investigation of the JFK assassination.

Suddenly Craig was offered a job in New Orleans as a personnel manager for an automobile firm owned by Willard Robertson, the chairman of a businessmen's committee that financed the Garrison investigation.

Then began another in a series of curious coincidences. On the night of December 22, 1967, Craig walked into his apartment in New Orleans just as a picture of Edgar Eugene Bradley, of North Hollywood, California, flashed on a television screen during a news broadcast. Garrison, the news announcer reported, had accused Bradley of conspiracy in the murder of John Kennedy.

Craig's heart started pounding. He said he turned to his wife and told her:

That's the man who identified himself as a Secret Service agent to me. I have always had that face in my mind. Everything that happened that day is a picture in my mind. I can remember his smooth complexion and cleft in his chin. I can remember every word said that day. . . .

Craig said he was absolutely certain that Bradley was the man he spoke with between "12:40 and 12:50 P.M." on the steps of the Texas Book Depository. He said he did not associate the "Secret Service agent" with the California man until he saw Bradley's image on the TV screen. Craig insisted that it was Bradley who mingled with Dallas police just after the assassination—telling the officers that he was in the United States Secret Service. Craig maintained that when he told Bradley how Oswald fled from the Book Depository in the Rambler station wagon, there was a singular lack of interest on Bradley's part.

Roger Craig swore in an affidavit that Bradley was the man he saw, and Jim Garrison asked Governor Ronald Reagan of California to extradite Edgar Eugene Bradley to Louisiana to stand trial as an accomplice in the murder of John Fitzgerald Kennedy.

Craig was not the only witness against Bradley. A New Orleans court clerk, Max Gonzales, testified that he had twice seen Bradley with another accused conspirator, David Ferrie, at the Lakefront Airport in New Orleans in "either June or July of

1963." According to Gonzales, the first time he saw Bradley and Ferrie together they were chatting in a restaurant at the airport. The second time, Gonzales said, Bradley was talking to Ferrie while the latter was doing mechanical work on an airplane.

In the normal course of events the cards might have been stacked against Edgar Eugene Bradley, who was associated with right-wing groups at the time of the JFK assassination, and indeed had been in Texas on November 22, 1963. However, Bradley maintained he was in El Paso and Anthony, Texas, on that day, and investigators for the California Attorney General's office bought his story and hinted to reporters that someone was trying to frame him. Governor Reagan denied Garrison's request for Bradley's extradition, and the D.A. was furious. He charged the "power structure" with thwarting his attempts to solve the JFK assassination. Garrison had made no secret of the fact that he was pointing the finger at the FBI and the CIA as prime movers behind the JFK assassination, and he strongly implied that their agents were lurking in the shadows, waiting to get him.

It is interesting to note that the intelligence files of the LAPD stated that "Edgar Eugene Bradley is the man Garrison mistook for Eugene Hale Brading."

This possibility intrigued Sergeant Chic Guitierrez of the Los Angeles Police SUS detail, for it almost appeared that Edgar Eugene Bradley was handed to Garrison by a faulty computer printout. And the obvious question, of course, was whether Eugene Hale Brading was the same man who represented himself to Roger Craig as a United States Secret Service agent in Dealey Plaza.

At the time of the JFK assassination, Gene Brading was forty-eight years old; Gene Bradley forty-three. Brading lived in Westwood, a Los Angeles suburb that is relatively close to Bradley's home in North Hollywood. In the opinion of Sergeant Chic Guitierrez, there was a strong facial resemblance between the two—strong enough to confuse a witness. Said Guitierrez: "I could look at these pictures [Brading and Bradley side by side] again in four or five years and I wouldn't be able to tell who was who—they look so much alike." The picture of Bradley displayed by Garrison was a profile shot, as was the photograph of Brading obtained by the LAPD from the Dallas widow whom he had married and bilked out of $50,000 in a matter of days.

At six feet two inches, Brading was a good five inches taller than Bradley. Originally, Roger Craig had testified that the Secret Service agent he talked to in Dealey Plaza was about six feet two inches tall. But after identifying Edgar Eugene Bradley as the man he saw in Dealey Plaza, Craig altered his testimony and said the man was about five feet ten inches tall, which, of course, matched Bradley's description. Both Brading and Bradley had long, wavy hair and ruddy complexions.

Originally, Roger Craig said the Secret Service agent had a large scar on his face. Gene Bradley had no scar, so Roger Craig retracted that part of his identification, which of course shot down much of his credibility. But Sergeant Guitierrez observed that while Gene Brading had no scar on his face, he did have a large scar on his right forearm.

Was that the scar Craig saw on the man in Dealey Plaza? Craig had lost his job as a deputy sheriff; he had been rebuffed by the Warren Commission, which classified him as a disputed witness. Now Jim Garrison was offering him sanctuary in New Orleans and a place in history.

Gene Bradley had no criminal record. He was an auxiliary policeman in Burbank, California. His credentials differed slightly from those of Gene Brading.

On the day of the assassination, Gene Brading was in Dallas by his own admission, admittedly using an assumed name. He was present in front of the Texas Book Depository, acting suspiciously. He was taken into custody and released, his inquisitors unaware of his true identity. Gene Brading had no double in Dealey Plaza. But apparently he needed one, and Jim Garrison found the perfect decoy, Edgar Eugene Bradley.

There was no problem tracking down Brading's presence in Dallas the day of the assassination. He was registered at one of Dallas' favorite mob hangouts, the Cabana Motel, one of the many enterprises financed by Jimmy Hoffa's Teamsters Union Pension Fund.

Bradley did not hesitate to admit that he was in Texas on November 22, 1963. He insisted he first went to El Paso, then to the city of Anthony, attempting to dispose of property willed to his employer, the Reverend Carl McIntyre, a spokesman of the extreme right wing.

The key witness against Bradley, according to Turner, was Dennis Mower, leader of the Southern California branch of the Minutemen, the fanatic, ultra-right-wing paramilitary organization that at one time had about one thousand members in the United States. Mower had testified that Gene Bradley offered him $10,000 to kill Senator John Kennedy in 1960 when Kennedy was campaigning for the presidency. Mower said he was to be paid $5,000 before the assassination, and another $5,000 after it was carried out.

According to Turner, Mower responded to Bradley, "I hate Kennedy but not enough to kill him."

At the time all this was supposed to have taken place, Dennis Mower would have been just fourteen years old, and I submit that people involved in assassination plots do not seek out the services of a boy passing through puberty.

The informant who supplied Garrison with the picture of Bradley that Roger Craig identified was Carol Aydelotte, who also lived in North Hollywood. Mrs. Aydelotte was known to Los Angeles police as a "den mother" to members of the

Minutemen and the American Nazi Party. Her husband, Art, was a member of both organizations and had once been arrested for having a large cache of weapons in his possession. For a time Dennis Mower lived with the Aydelottes, and he became a gun-runner under their tutelage. And another coincidence to cope with: one of Mower's closest friends was Philip Earl Scheib, son of the cut-rate car-painter who ran with the Brading-Pereira crowd.

Another factor that, according to Turner, led Garrison to accuse Edgar Eugene Bradley was the testimony of two women whose names I was not able to obtain.

Supposedly, a woman who once lived next door to Bradley said that when he returned home from his trip to Texas after the JFK assassination, she told him in jest: "Gene, if I didn't know you so well I'd say you did it."

The woman quoted Bradley as replying: "I didn't, but I know who did."

The woman also told the Garrison investigator she once overheard a violent confrontation inside the Bradley home, which sits on a pleasant, tree-shaded street in North Hollywood. She said Bradley was beating his teen-age son, and she distinctly heard the youth shout, "Dad, I don't care how bad he was. You shouldn't have killed him."

The Garrison plot thickened when the woman said she saw Clay Shaw and Colonel William Gale visit the Bradley home. Shaw, of course, was identified by Garrison as a coconspirator in the JFK assassination. Colonel Gale, a frequent candidate for public office in California, was identified by the California Attorney General as a right-wing paramilitary activist. Among the organizations Gale led was the California Rangers, which had much in common with the Minutemen. While Edgar Eugene Bradley was connected with a number of right-wing causes, he was never a member of any paramilitary organization to the best knowledge of police intelligence agencies in California, which made a habit of infiltrating such organizations in the days before they were forced to focus all their attention on the radical left.

Bradley, in fact, was a bitter enemy of the Minutemen and had even gotten into a running feud with members of the John Birch Society in the San Fernando Valley. Perhaps that was his undoing.

The other woman who ostensibly figured in the Garrison indictment lived in Tulsa, Oklahoma. Bradley had stopped off at her house before taking a bus to Anthony, Texas, the day of the assassination. The woman told Garrison's investigators she observed several weapons in Bradley's suitcase when he opened it inside her house.

That was Garrison's *prima facie* case against Edgar Eugene Bradley.

My investigation convinced me that the case against Bradley was a fraud; that perhaps the LAPD intelligence files had been correct when they stated that Bradley was the man Garrison had mistaken for Eugene Hale Brading. I wondered if it were an honest mistake or if Garrison had some ulterior motive.

But the damage had been done to one individual. One day I telephoned Bradley and requested an interview. He agreed and I went to his neighborhood but somehow knocked on the wrong door.

An elderly man answered, and I asked if he could direct me to Gene Bradley's house. He responded, "Oh, you mean the guy who killed Kennedy. He lives a couple of doors down the street on the next block."

Such was the impact of the Garrison investigation, at least in its initial stages.

VIII

WHERE IT ALL BEGAN

On February 16, 1967, reporter Rosemary James of the *New Orleans States-Item* disclosed the first details of Jim Garrison's investigation into the assassination of President Kennedy and, in so doing, touched off a tidal wave of curiosity. Newspaper, radio, and television reporters from all over the world swarmed into New Orleans, bracing themselves for sensational disclosures. And at first, they were not to be disappointed.

After all, hadn't Lee Harvey Oswald lived in New Orleans prior to the JFK assassination? And hadn't this one-time defector to the Soviet Union taken part in the Communist-inspired activities of the Fair Play for Cuba Committee? It had all begun in the land of the Mardi Gras, so why shouldn't it end there?

The Gallup Poll showed that the majority of the American people desperately wanted to believe in Jim Garrison, a hulking figure of a man who had whetted their appetite with the advancement of a conspiracy theory in the JFK assassination. At first glance, the towering Garrison seemed to have

the credibility of a Lincoln. He had a reputation
for taking on all comers in New Orleans, including
Criminal Court judges, and usually winning.
Newsmen checking into New Orleans were advised never to underestimate "Big Jim."

In a series of interviews Garrison speculated
about the possible forces behind the assassination,
singling out such diverse groups as right-wing extremists, anti-Castro Cubans, Cubans in general,
the FBI, the CIA, the "military-industrial complex," and "other."

Gradually word about the D.A.'s probe leaked
out and the plot thickened. Garrison identified
the major culprits as socialite-businessman Clay
Shaw, the retired director of the International
Trade Mart, a nonprofit corporation formed to
promote world trade through the Port of New
Orleans, and David William Ferrie, a brilliant but
extremely odd individual and a notorious homosexual. At the time Shaw was fifty-four; Ferrie
forty-nine.

Ferrie was considered Garrison's most significant catch. Shortly after the JFK assassination he
was questioned about a possible relationship with
Oswald by both the FBI and Secret Service, then
cleared of any complicity in the crime. Ferrie had
been an outstanding pilot for Eastern Airlines for
ten years but had been fired because of his homosexual activities.

But more significant than all the folderol about
Ferrie's past, which Garrison played up so prominently, is the fact that on the day John Kennedy's

blood was shed in Dealey Plaza, Ferrie's name was mentioned almost immediately.

At that time David Ferrie was a personal investigator for Carlos Marcello, a squat Mafia chieftain who ruled his territory in the southeastern United States with an iron hand. If any man had reason for wanting the Kennedy brothers killed, it was Carlos Marcello, who claimed he had been kidnapped at their instigation and flown out of the country.

Not once during the New Orleans investigation did Jim Garrison allude to Ferrie's ties to Marcello and the possibility that organized crime could have masterminded the assassination. Instead Garrison chose to depict Ferrie as a "right-wing radical" who plotted with anti-Castro Cuban extremists. That very well may have been an accurate description of one side of Ferrie. But the other side was a man who served the Brotherhood and served it well. David Ferrie worked for the Mafia by his own admission.

So it seems strange that Carlos Marcello let his most trusted investigator fall into Jim Garrison's legal straightjacket. It is no secret in New Orleans that Garrison and Marcello are friends. So if the investigation was a sham, as United States Attorney General Ramsey Clark and countless others contended, why didn't Marcello try to intervene on Ferrie's behalf? Marcello had once tried to intervene with a bribe on behalf of his good friend Jimmy Hoffa. And Ferrie had done much more for Marcello than Hoffa.

Perhaps David Ferrie had become expendable? He knew more about Marcello than anyone else in the organization. And as a homosexual, Ferrie was extremely vulnerable. He had been showing increasing symptoms of instability, and perhaps David Ferrie was a marked man.

In the early stages of the investigation Garrison made no mention of Edgar Eugene Bradley. But he frequently made sinister references to unnamed coconspirators, some of whom, he alleged, were present in Dealey Plaza when John Kennedy was murdered.

The sensational nature of the D.A.'s probe struck like a rapier. Garrison's investigators marched into Clay Shaw's baroque dwelling and emerged triumphantly with an assortment of whips, robes, and other bizarre playthings that implied that the silver-haired businessman had a certain demoniacal quality.

There was nothing much in the body of evidence that could link Clay Shaw to Lee Harvey Oswald, despite Garrison's contention that the killer of the President knew Shaw under the name of "Clay Bertrand." The chief witness against Shaw was Vernon Bundy, a twenty-seven-year-old black who happened to be a narcotics addict. Bundy admitted he took four "caps" of heroin daily. Bundy said that one morning in the summer of 1963 he was about to take a "pop" on the shore of Lake Pontchartrain, near New Orleans, when he saw Clay Shaw hand Oswald a "wad" of money.

107

Asked by Shaw's lawyer how he supported his expensive heroin habit, Bundy answered, "I steal sometimes."

Other witnesses produced by Garrison were equally dubious. According to Garrison, one of his critical witnesses was a twenty-five-year-old insurance salesman named Perry Raymond Russo. According to the D.A., Russo knew Ferrie well and had once heard him say that President Kennedy should have been killed for bungling the Bay of Pigs invasion. Also, according to Garrison, Russo had knowledge of a conspiracy meeting in Ferrie's apartment attended by both Shaw and Oswald.

But Garrison's credibility suffered a setback when James Phalen, a writer for the *Saturday Evening Post*, discovered documents in the D.A.'s own office that showed Russo had had no knowledge of an assassination plot or of a meeting at Ferrie's apartment until the time he was given sodium pentothal, the so-called truth serum. Phalen reported that Dr. Esmond Fatter put Russo in a hypnotic state—at Garrison's direction —and told him to picture a television screen on which he would see "Bertrand, Ferrie, and Oswald . . . and they are talking about assassinating someone." At first Phalen's story seemed incredible. District Attorneys just don't behave that way. But then it was confirmed that Russo had indeed been hypnotized—just a few hours before a scheduled pretrial appearance called by Garrison.

Garrison was wrong about Clay Shaw and Edgar Eugene Bradley. The case against them was a monumental fraud. But both were convenient for Garrison's purposes—Shaw because of his personal vulnerability, Bradley perhaps because of his name and physical characteristics.

Although there was positive evidence that David Ferrie had known Oswald, despite the disclaimers of Warren Commission investigators, it didn't make much difference. On February 22, 1967, six days after the *New Orleans States-Item* disclosed what Garrison was up to, Ferrie's body was found in his apartment, which was littered with newspaper clippings, magazine articles, and diagrams relating to the JFK assassination.

The coroner of New Orleans, Dr. Nicholas Chetta, said Ferrie died of a ruptured blood vessel in his brain. At first, Garrison said it was murder. Then he pronounced that Ferrie had killed himself because his involvement in the JFK assassination was known at last. At this point, a sort of mass hysteria was starting to build once more among the American people. It was symbolized by an editorial cartoon by Paul Conrad, the Pulitzer Prize winner, which showed persons dropping dead all over New Orleans, just as they had in Dallas after the JFK assassination.

That may have been the zenith of Garrison's career. His credibility was never better. He seemed to be beaming when he called a news conference in New Orleans and told reporters:

The apparent suicide of David Ferrie ends the life of a man who, in my judgment, was one of history's most important individuals. Evidence developed by our office has long since confirmed that he was involved in events culminating in the assassination of President Kennedy. Apparently, we waited too long.

Although Ferrie was dead, Garrison gave the impression that he was intensifying his investigation. He maintained that Ferrie was the man selected to fly the getaway plane for Lee Harvey Oswald and his coconspirators. It was simply a matter of tying up the loose ends. Clay Shaw would have his day in court, and so would Edgar Eugene Bradley.

Then Garrison started talking about his "new evidence." He maintained that Edgar Eugene Bradley had been active in New Orleans, plotting the assassination with Shaw, Ferrie, and Oswald, and the D.A. obtained a Grand Jury indictment to that effect.

I called Garrison's office and asked an aide about the language of the indictment. Did it specify the date on which the conspiracy allegedly took place?

"Yes it did," the Garrison aide told me. "The indictment says the meeting took place in the middle of September in 1963." It was difficult for me to believe that the indictment was not more precise. If there was such a meeting and witnesses were present, wasn't it logical that the exact date would be spelled out in the indictment? Wouldn't the witnesses at least know what day of the week the meeting took place?

"No," the Garrison aide said. "We don't do things that way down here."

Every time Garrison opened his mouth in the days after Ferrie's death, his appearance of credibility appeared to be giving way to one of lunacy. Perhaps the most perceptive observer of the circus in New Orleans was Hugh Aynesworth, of *Newsweek* magazine. Writing in the May 15, 1967, edition of *Newsweek*, Aynesworth had this to say about the Garrison investigation:

> Jim Garrison is right. There has been a conspiracy in New Orleans—but it is a plot of Garrison's own making. It is a scheme to concoct a fantastic "solution" to the death of John F. Kennedy, and to make it stick; in this cause the district attorney and his staff have been parties to the death of one man and have humiliated, harassed and financially gutted several others.

Aynesworth accused Garrison of offering $3,000 and a job with an airline to Alan Beauboeuf, a supposed friend of Ferrie, to testify that he overheard the planning of the JFK assassination. And Aynesworth continued:

> I also know that when the D.A.'s office learned this entire bribery attempt had been tape-recorded, two of Garrison's men re-

turned to the "witness" [Beauboeuf], and he says, threatened him with physical harm.

Another man who spent many hours with the District Attorney in a vain attempt to dissuade him from his assassination-conspiracy theory has twice been threatened—once by the D.A.'s own "witnesses," the second time by Garrison himself.

That was one view of the Garrison investigation. Hugh Aynesworth may have been right in stating that there was a "plot" of Garrison's own making, but the reasons for it may have been far more subtle than they appeared on the surface.

From the start, Garrison was prepared for the role of martyr if he got caught in his own crossfire. In an interview with *Playboy* magazine he said, "I was perfectly aware that I might have signed my political death warrant the moment I launched this case—but I couldn't care less as long as I could shed some light on John Kennedy's assassination."

Despite what Garrison said, his moves against David Ferrie appeared designed to create an element of doubt. He set up a straw man, destroyed him, then walked away from the macabre scene. Why was Jim Garrison the architect of his own political downfall? Why had he picked David Ferrie as the instrument of that self-destruction?

Ferrie was a strange individual, a New Orleans curiosity. He was bald and had no eyebrows (reportedly because of burns), so he covered up his hairless spots with pasted-on mohair. In his youth Ferrie had studied to be a Catholic priest. He read Latin and Greek and spoke fluent Spanish. He was listed in the New Orleans city directory as a psychiatrist, although he had no degree nor any formal education in that field. His real skill was that of a hypnotist. His powers of persuasion were said to be uncanny.

One CIA agent who was assigned to Lee Harvey Oswald for a time was convinced that Ferrie placed the President's assassin in a hypnotic trance; that Oswald actually had no idea of the tragedy he had brought about when he walked out of the Texas Book Depository on November 22, 1963. At best that would appear to be a highly doubtful theory, despite Ferrie's ability as a hypnotist.

Ferrie feared death. After Garrison's investigators started staking out his apartment, he was observed pacing back and forth in his living room hour after hour. Carlos Marcello made no attempt to shield him, even though a mere whistle from the Mafia boss would have called off the wolves.

Shortly before Garrison planned to charge him with murder, friends reported that Ferrie was terrified and that he had no idea why he was under constant surveillance. They said he went to the D.A. and asked for physical protection against unnamed persons. After several days in protective custody he returned to his apartment, where he was found dead seventy-two hours later.

In his apartment, police found an unsigned, undated note which said, "To leave this life is, for me, a sweet prospect. I find nothing in it that is desirable and on the other hand everything that is loathsome."

About a week after Ferrie's death, *Newsweek* writer Aynesworth interviewed Garrison at his home. He quoted the D.A. as admitting to him: "Yeah, we killed the son of a bitch."

Since Ferrie was dead and Governor Reagan refused to extradite Edgar Eugene Bradley from California to stand trial on the conspiracy charges, Clay Shaw was the only sitting duck left in Garrison's shooting gallery.

The trial was a sham; it was perhaps the most disgraceful legal event of the twentieth century. The jury wasted no time in finding Shaw not guilty. Many of Garrison's colleagues in the legal profession demanded that he be impeached. Yet in 1969, shortly after the trial, he was elected for a third term as District Attorney of New Orleans.

The most significant thing Garrison did at the trial was to show the Zapruder film of the assassination to the jury. "That," he crowed, "proves there was a conspiracy."

If indeed Garrison planted the seeds of his own destruction, there must have been a reason for it. To evaluate properly what happened in New Orleans, one must refocus on the events that took place in Dealey Plaza on November 22, 1963.

IX

WHY FERRIE?

In the hours that followed the assassination it was difficult to determine who was making the most progress in the investigation—law-enforcement officers or the press.

The only known recorded interview with Lee Harvey Oswald was made on film by John Hart, then a reporter for CBS television station KNXT, in Los Angeles. The Dallas police made not one transcription of their interviews with Oswald. Hart had mislaid his press card and was carrying nothing to identify himself as a member of the working press when he arrived in Dallas several hours after John Kennedy was gunned down in Dealey Plaza. Yet he somehow managed to maneuver himself and his camera crew into a position where they could interview Oswald as he was being shuttled about in the Dallas police headquarters. The interview was brief and to the point. Oswald flatly denied that he murdered John Kennedy. The fact that Hart managed to interview Oswald disputes the claim of Captain Will Fritz, of the Dallas Police Homicide Bureau, who insisted that all access to Oswald was cut off while the assassin was being interrogated, that Deputy Sheriff Roger Craig could not possibly have been in the same room as Oswald, and that Craig could not have heard Oswald say, "Everybody will know who I am now."

Reporters and cameramen for NBC News swarmed over Dallas, gathering information, some of which appeared to be significant.

When Jim Garrison first focused public attention on David Ferrie in New Orleans, he acted as if he had made a monumental discovery. But in fact, an obscure reference to Ferrie can be found in the Warren report—in Volume XXIV, Exhibit 2038, which is a report of an interview of NBC cameraman Gene Barnes by FBI agents Eugene P. Pittman and John C. Oakes.

> Barnes said Bob Mulholland, NBC News, Chicago, talked in Dallas to one Fairy [sic], a narcotics addict now out on bail on a sodomy charge in Dallas. Fairy said that Oswald had been under hynopsis from a man doing a mind-reading act at Ruby's "Carousel." Fairy was said to be a private detective and the owner of an airplane who took young boys on flights "just for kicks." Mulholland may be located at Room 1537, Statler Hotel, Dallas . . . or through his Chicago headquarters.

Barnes's description of Ferrie, as apparently conveyed to him by Mulholland, appeared accurate. There were strong indications that Ferrie dabbled in narcotics, and his homosexual activities had long been a matter of public record on police blotters. It was not true, however, that he was out on bail on a sodomy charge in Dallas. Barnes was willing to concede that some of his information about Ferrie was slightly garbled, but the basic facts were correct. The question is: how and why did Gene Barnes know so much about David Ferrie so early in the assassination investigation, particularly since Ferrie's name was anything but a household word?

At this writing Bob Mulholland is a top executive with NBC News in New York City. In an interview with me in Los Angeles Mulholland insisted he had been quoted incorrectly in the Warren report. He said that shortly after the assassination he heard FBI agents mention Ferrie's name and a possible link to Oswald, and he relayed that information to his reporters in Dallas.

In any event, it is quite obvious that Jim Garrison did not discover David Ferrie, that Ferrie was initially discovered by the FBI, but that for reasons not yet answered—at least to my satisfaction—Ferrie escaped the type of scrutiny he deserved because of his ties to Mafioso Carlos Marcello.

Several other members of NBC News who covered the events in Dallas told me they were convinced their superiors wanted certain evidence suppressed at the request of someone in Washington, D.C. Having been in television news for many years, I am always skeptical of such claims—although I must admit that the words *investigative reporting* often strike fear in the hearts of network-television executives, who oversee the news business by virtue of their ability to sell advertising time to purveyors of soup, soap or aspirin.

However, one former member of an NBC camera team that had been in Dallas told me, "An FBI agent said that I should never discuss what we discovered [about the assassination] for the good of the country."

The further testimony of NBC cameraman Gene Barnes in Volume XXIV of the Warren report may shed some light on that "discovery."

Barnes was told by one Bogard, salesman for Downtown Lincoln-Mercury, Dallas, that about two weeks prior to the Oswald shooting, he gave Oswald a demonstration ride in a Comet automobile, which ride covered about seventeen miles instead of the usual twelve or fourteen blocks. Bogard said Oswald drove, accelerating on expressways, decelerating in city traffic, and indicating he knew where he wanted to drive. Oswald refused to sign any papers, saying he wanted to pay cash for the car, the price of which was $3,500.00, and that he would be back in about ten days to pay cash. He gave Bogard

the name of Lee Oswald and Bogard gave
him a business card.

This was part of the testimony in the Warren
report that convinced a few of its critics that there
must have been a "second Oswald," since Lee
Harvey Oswald, it was thought, did not know how
to drive. But the information developed by NBC
News indicated that Oswald was indeed the
driver and that the car he picked out—a red
Comet—was the type of vehicle favored by
William David Ferrie, who owned a blue Comet.

Furthermore, the NBC newsmen learned that
the ride apparently took Oswald over the exact
route traveled by President Kennedy's motorcade
on November 22, 1963. But since the presidential
route in Dallas had not been published two weeks
before the assassination, those in charge of the
NBC operation had second thoughts: Oswald apparently never took a ride in a red Comet; David
Ferrie was simply a red herring.

Ultimately the Warren Commission checked
into the story and, while admitting there was
corroborating testimony about the ride in the
Comet, decided to dismiss it from the body of
hard evidence.

This is how the Commission evaluated it:

The testimony of Albert Guy Bogard has
been carefully evaluated because it suggests
the possibility that Oswald might have been
a proficient automobile driver and, during No-

vember 1963, might have been expecting funds with which to purchase a car. Bogard, formerly a salesman with a Lincoln-Mercury firm in Dallas, testified that in the early afternoon of November 9, 1963, he attended a prospective customer who he believes was Lee Harvey Oswald. According to Bogard, the customer, after test driving an automobile over the Stemmons Freeway at 60 to 70 miles per hour, told Bogard that in several weeks he would have the money to make a purchase. Bogard asserted that the customer gave his name as "Lee Oswald," which Bogard wrote on a business card. After Oswald's name was mentioned on radio on November 22, Bogard assertedly threw the card in a trash can, making the comment to co-employes that Oswald would no longer wish to buy a car.

Bogard's testimony has received corroboration. The assistant sales manager at the time, Frank Pizzo, and a second salesman, Eugene M. Wilson, stated that they recall an instance when the customer described by Bogard was in the showroom. Another salesman, Oran Brown, recalled that Bogard asked him to assist the customer if he appeared during certain evenings when Bogard was away from the showroom. Brown stated that he too wrote down the customer's name and both he and his wife remember the name

"Oswald" as being on a paper in his possession before the assassination.

However, doubts exist about the accuracy of Bogard's testimony. He, Pizzo, and Wilson differed on important details of what is supposed to have occurred when the customer was in the showroom. Whereas Bogard stated that the customer said he did not wish credit and wanted to purchase a car for cash, Pizzo and Wilson both indicated that the man did attempt to purchase on credit. According to Wilson, when the customer was told he would be unable to purchase a car without a credit rating, substantial cash or a lengthy employment record, he stated sarcastically, "Maybe I'm going to have to go back to Russia to buy a car." While it is possible that Oswald would have made such a remark, the statement is not consistent with Bogard's story. Indeed, Bogard made no mention that the customer ever spoke with Wilson while he was in the showroom. More important, on November 23, a search through the showroom's refuse was made, but no paper bearing Oswald's name was found. The paper on which Brown reportedly wrote Oswald's name has never been located.

The assistant sales manager, Mr. Pizzo, who saw Bogard's prospect on November 9 and shortly after the assassination felt that Oswald may have been the man, later examined pictures of Oswald and expressed serious doubts that the person with Bogard was in fact Oswald. While noting a resemblance, he did not believe that Oswald's hairline matched that of the person who had been in the showroom on November 9. Wilson has stated that Bogard's customer was only about 5 feet tall. Several persons who knew Oswald have testified that he was unable to drive, although Mrs. [Ruth] Paine, who was giving Oswald driving lessons, stated that Oswald was showing some improvement by November. Moreover, Oswald's whereabouts on November 9, as testified to by Marina Oswald and Ruth Paine, would have made it impossible for him to have visited the automobile showrooms as Mr. Bogard claims.

Note that the Commission did not mention the type of car Oswald was alleged to have driven, nor did it note the proximity—easy walking distance—of the Lincoln-Mercury dealership to the Texas Book Depository.

Time and time again the Commission appeared to use the same tactics to avoid the possibility of developing evidence that might lead to a conspiracy. Yet students of history can be thankful that at least the Commission laid most of the evidence before the public.

The other question still unanswered is: why did David Ferrie, according to NBC cameraman Gene Barnes, attempt to link Oswald to a hypnotist performing at Jack Ruby's Carousel? Was he attempting to divert attention from himself and his own hypnotic abilities, which were legend in New Orleans? Was Ferrie in Dallas shortly after the assassination? It would appear so, simply from what Barnes is quoted as saying in the Warren report. Ferrie, on the other hand, maintained that on the day of the assassination he left New Orleans for Houston to hunt geese with two young men.

While FBI agents in Dallas apparently ignored Ferrie's story—they did not even bother to interview Bob Mulholland, or so the record indicates—their counterparts in New Orleans were actively pursuing the story for their own reasons.

There was a frantic effort to determine Ferrie's whereabouts around the period of the assassination. The fact that Ferrie was actually interviewed by FBI and Secret Service agents in New Orleans about a possible link to Oswald was withheld from the body of evidence presented in the Warren report's twenty-six volumes for reasons that have never been made clear.

But when Jim Garrison started to make waves in New Orleans, the government placed in evidence a document from the National Archives to prove that the claims of a possible Oswald-Ferrie relationship had been thoroughly investigated after the assassination and had been determined to be unfounded. The tactical move against Garrison was made by United States Attorney General Ramsey Clark, who reportedly considered it his duty to protect the integrity of the Warren Commission's investigation. But the question at this point is: why was the report omitted from the main body of evidence presented to the public by the Warren Commission? And one must wonder what other information was suppressed.

The Secret Service document dealing with the Oswald-Ferrie investigation was placed in the National Archives on February 23, 1967, the day after David William Ferrie's body was found in his New Orleans apartment. It is a document worthy of detailed examination for what it says, and for what it does not say.

X

THE TRAIL TO MARCELLO

Did the FBI know something about a possible Oswald-Ferrie relationship and try to cover it up, or did the bureau simply disregard the information it had collected because it did not seem significant in the eyes of Warren Commission attorneys? Bob Mulholland, of NBC News, insisted that he first learned about Ferrie from the FBI, which had linked him to Oswald shortly after John Kennedy was assassinated. Ramsey Clark found it convenient to release a long-suppressed report about David Ferrie at the time of the Garrison investigation. Clark apparently thought it was significant that Ferrie had been questioned as a suspect and then released, but the Attorney General did not seem to see the importance of the questions the report left unanswered or the fact that no government agents had disproved an Oswald-Ferrie relationship.

From the start of the investigation in Dallas, the late FBI Director, J. Edgar Hoover, appeared to be an intensely angry man. Hoover yanked the FBI agent who had been assigned to Oswald in

Dallas out of the city so quickly after the assassination that he didn't have time to put a "for sale" sign in front of his home. Then there was the story of Richard Nagell, the CIA agent who claimed to have written a letter to Hoover before the assassination, warning him that Oswald intended to kill the President. Nagell, it was reported, had knowledge of a conspiracy and of the Oswald-Ferrie relationship.

It seemed apparent during the early stages of the investigation in Dallas that David Ferrie's trail was somewhat circuitous but that it very possibly led to Oswald and very definitely ended on the doorstep of Carlos Marcello.

The FBI and Secret Service went through the motions, and that was about all. After the Warren report was issued, it was clear that no importance was attached to David William Ferrie, to the mysterious "Jim Braden," or to certain other curiosities that developed during the course of the investigation. The American public was spoon-fed the evidence as it was laid out in the Warren Commission's twenty-six volumes. And perhaps, in 1965, that was as much as it could swallow.

But then Jim Garrison got up on his soap box in New Orleans, and Attorney General Ramsey Clark reacted in hair-trigger fashion. Despite Clark's original intent—the aborting of the Garrison investigation—he helped provide some of the most important clues in this investigation by making a public document out of a Secret Service report that showed Ferrie to be working for the Mafia at the time of the assassination.

The report revealed that Ferrie had been doing investigative work for Marcello. Further investigation showed that Ferrie had also been Marcello's pilot.

The day after the JFK slaying, word about a possible Oswald-Ferrie relationship filtered into the office of the United States Secret Service in New Orleans. The next day, November 24, 1963, Special Agents John W. Rice and Anthony E. Gerrots began an investigation that lasted five days.

They summarized their investigation this way:

> Investigation disclosed that information furnished by Jack S. Martin to the effect that David William Ferrie associated with Lee Harvey Oswald and trained Oswald in the use of a rifle with telescopic sight, also that Ferrie had visited Dallas several weeks prior to the assassination of President John F. Kennedy is without foundation. Jack S. Martin, who has the appearance of being an alcoholic, has the reputation locally of furnishing incorrect information to law enforcement officers, attorneys, etc.

Jack S. Martin was a New Orleans private detective who perhaps knew David Ferrie better than any other man. Martin was a bishop in a strange religious cult known as the Old Catholic

Church of North America. He had ordained Ferrie as a bishop in the cult, but he was not a homosexual, as Ferrie was. Both Martin and Ferrie had been active in the anti-Castro movement, which also happened to be a pet project of la Cosa Nostra, since organized crime had lost its foothold in Cuba—along with the lush gambling revenue from Havana's casinos—when the Communists took power.

Martin and another private detective, the late W. Guy Bannister, had set up the Cuban Revolutionary Council, which operated out of a building at 544 Camp Street, New Orleans. Perhaps it is just another coincidence, but Oswald used the address of 544 Camp Street on literature he distributed on behalf of the left-leaning Fair Play for Cuba Committee.

Bannister's connections with the far right were said to go much deeper than his anti-Castro activities. A former FBI agent, Bannister was reported to be a leading figure in the southeastern branch of the Minutemen, the same fanatical organization that had helped Jim Garrison link Edgar Eugene Bradley to the assassination "plot."

The Warren Commission was somewhat stumped by the fact that Oswald had picked the Camp Street address as his base of operations. So the Commission solved the problem by writing, ". . . neither the Fair Play for Cuba Committee nor Lee Harvey Oswald ever maintained an office at that address."

The convoluted path in New Orleans was just

Latest U.S. Government
tests of all cigarettes
show True is
lower in both
tar and nicotine
than 98% of all other
cigarettes sold.

Think about it.
Shouldn't your next cigarette be True?

Regular: 12 mg. "tar", 0.7 mg. nicotine,
Menthol: 12 mg. "tar", 0.8 mg. nicotine, av. per cigarette, FTC Report Feb. '73.

Latest U.S. Government
tests of all menthol
cigarettes show
True is lower
in both tar and
nicotine than 98% of
all other menthols sold.

Think about it.
Shouldn't your next cigarette be True?

© Lorillard 1973

as difficult to follow as it was in Dallas. But it is obvious that Dallas and New Orleans are interlocking parts in the mechanism of any legitimate investigation of the JFK assassination.

Jack Martin originally conveyed his information about Ferrie to the United States Secret Service via an anonymous route. In detailing their investigation, Secret Service agents Rice and Gerrots wrote:

At 5:00 P.M. on 11-24-63 Donald Mitchell, 1501½ General Taylor St., New Orleans (rear basement apartment), called at the office and was interviewed by a reporting agent. Mr. Mitchell stated that he shares an apartment with one J. Philip Stein, a/k/a "Jerry." Mr. Mitchell advised also that the telephone in this apartment is in the name of Herman S. Kohlman, Assistant District Attorney, Parish of Orleans, New Orleans, La., for the reason that Mr. Kohlman formerly shared the apartment with J. Philip Stein, but that Kohlman recently married and moved from the apartment. The telephone number in question is Twinbrook 1-8703. During the interview with Mr. Mitchell he stated that some time during the afternoon of Sunday 11-24-63 Jerry Stein answered the telephone in their apartment; that the person calling was endeavoring to contact Herman S. Kohlman, explaining to Stein that the reason he was trying to get in touch with Kohlman was that Kohlman had written a story about an individual known as "Farry;" that "Farry" was a hypnotist and had either taught or had something to do with Oswald being taught how to use rifles with telescopic lenses, also indicating that "Farry" had been in Dallas about two weeks prior to 11-24-63 and that "Farry" had been corresponding with Oswald. According to Mr. Mitchell, the person making this telephone call said his name was "Jack" —no last name given. Subsequent to the interview with Donald Mitchell, several attempts were made to contact Herman S. Kolhman.

At 11:00 P.M. on 11-24-63 a telephone call was received from J. Philip Stein. He stated he did not know "Jack's" last name. He stated that he was told by "Jack" that "Farry" had been training some Civil Air Patrol boys in the use of foreign made arms and allegedly trained Oswald in the use of a rifle.

Stein stated that "Farry" is said to be rather intelligent; that he allegedly has a PhD and is a hypnotist. He said that Herman S. Kohlman, a former newspaper reporter, had written a story about "Farry" about two years ago and that the story had appeared in the *Times-Picayune*, a New Orleans newspaper. Stein stated that according to "Jack," "Farry" is alleged to have been communicating with Oswald and that both were allegedly engaged in the same type of work.

He said that "Farry" was believed to be living in the Louisiana Parkway area, New Orleans.

At 11:10 P.M. on 11-24-63 reporting agent received a telephone call from Herman S. Kohlman. He said that he was an assistant District Attorney.

At this point Kohlman identified "Farry" as David William Ferrie, and advised the Secret Service agents that Ferrie had been arrested several times on charges of committing morals offenses against young boys.

Here is the Secret Service's record of what Kohlman told them:

He said that Ferrie at one time lived on Atherton Drive in Montairio, La., a suburb of New Orleans. Mr. Kohlman stated that at the time of his conversation with me his office had ten Police Officers (investigators for the District Attorney's office) scouring the city for David Ferrie and that in the event Ferrie was picked up he would notify me. (No request of Mr. Kohlman was made that Ferrie be picked up and held for this service.)

At 12:35 A.M. on 11-25-63 Assistant District Attorney Herman S. Kohlman telephoned the reporting agent at his residence, at which time he advised that David William Ferrie had left for Dallas 11-22-63 during the afternoon, traveling in a light blue Comet.

He also advised that Ferrie reportedly had a plane and may still have it. He said that at the time of his telephone conversation with me Ferrie was allegedly on his way back to New Orleans.

Mr. Kohlman stated that it was his information that Harvey Lee Oswald [sic] was in Ferrie's Civil Air Patrol group in New Orleans some years ago; that Ferrie allegedly had a fraudulent charter and that the Civil Aeronautics Board checked on it.

When pressed for the full name of the informant thus far referred to only as "Jack," Mr. Kohlman stated that he was "just a fellow who worked around the police headquarters building" and that "Jack" did not want to become involved in this investigation and for that reason did not want his name mentioned in any way. Mr. Kohlman was informed that "Jack" would have to be interviewed in person by representatives of this service.

During the late afternoon of 11-25-63 SAIC [Special Agent in Charge] Rice received a telephone call from Herman S. Kohlman, advising that David Ferrie had been picked up by representatives of the Orleans Parish District Attorney's office at that time.

Mr. Kohlman informed SAIC Rice that Ferrie would shortly be brought to the First

District Police Station where he would be booked.

At this point in the narrative, Secret Service agents Rice and Gerrots decided it would be in their own best interests to interview the mystery man named David Ferrie, so they took the initiative, unaware that the FBI was already involved in the same investigation in New Orleans.

Excerpting again from the report:

David William Ferrie stated that when he was employed by Eastern Air Lines he flew mostly to Houston, San Antonio, Corpus Christi and Brownsville and various intermediate points; that he sometimes flew to New York via Atlanta and Washington.

Ferrie insisted that he was in New Orleans on Thursday, November 21, 1963 and on Friday, November 22, 1963 until about 9:00 P.M. He said that he is positive that he was in New Orleans on the dates mentioned because he had been in court in connection with a trial involving Carlos Marcello. He said that he departed New Orleans about 9:00 P.M. on 11-22-63 and drove to Houston, Texas, with two companions, Alvin Beauboeuf, about 19 or 20 years old, of 2427 Alvar St., New Orleans, and Melvin Coffey, about 26 or 28 years old, 618 N. Pierce St., New Orleans; that he was driving a 1961 blue Comet 4-door station wagon with 1963 Louisiana license, having bought the car from Delta Mercury, Inc., 2201 Canal St., New Orleans, about three or four weeks previously —Charles Graham, salesman.

I believe a parenthetical observation is needed at this point: the man known as Jim Braden also gave his destination as Houston, Texas, on November 22, 1963.

Ferrie stated that he and his two companions mentioned above returned to New Orleans about 9:30 P.M. on 11-24-63; that he telephoned Attorney G. Wray Gill (by whom he is employed as an investigator) several times; that at Gill's suggestion he left New Orleans about midnight that same date and drove to Hammond, La., alone, where he stayed at the Holloway Smith Hall on Sycamore Street, at the Southeastern Louisiana College, where he has a friend, Thomas Compton, who does research in narcotics addiction under a Doctor Nichols under a federal grant.

Another observation: Ferrie was described in the Warren report as a narcotics addict. Was that the reason Attorney Gill dispatched him to Southeastern Louisiana College?

He said he left Hammond about 1 P.M. on 11-25-63 and arrived in New Orleans about

3 P.M.; that immediately upon arriving at New Orleans he contacted Attorney Gill, who accompanied him to the Orleans Parish District Attorney's office, where he was wanted for questioning in connection with the Oswald case.

There seemed to be a game plan to what was happening. Why was it so crucial that Ferrie went to the college where his friend did research in narcotics addiction? At that point he was wanted for questioning, presumably by the FBI as well as Assistant District Attorney Kohlman. The Secret Service report stated:

> During the interview with Ferrie by SAIC Rice and myself he stated that he had left New Orleans on 10-11-63 via Taca Air Lines for Guatemala, returning via the same route, arriving New Orleans on 10-18-63. He stated that he again left New Orleans on 10-30-63 via Taca Air Lines for Guatemala for Attorney G. Wray Gill and the trips involved some investigative work having to do with the Carlos Marcello case.

Why, at this point in the interview, did the Secret Service agents bring up the subject of Carlos Marcello from out of the blue? It appears that they were the ones who pursued the matter of Ferrie's relationship with the Mafia chieftain. Being resident agents in New Orleans, they must have been aware of the bitter hatred Marcello had for the Kennedy family, particularly Robert Kennedy, who was then serving his brother as Attorney General.

Marcello maintained that he had once been kidnapped by Bobby Kennedy and flown off to Guatemala. The animosity Marcello harbored for the Kennedys was public knowledge in New Orleans. It is also important to note that Marcello was a close ally of another embattled enemy of the Kennedys, former Teamsters Union President James R. Hoffa. Were the Secret Service agents, in pursuing this line of questioning with Ferrie, trying to corroborate any suspicions they might have had concerning Carlos Marcello and the assassination? If not, the references to Marcello and the trips to Guatemala seem to pop up as non sequiturs in the investigation.

In the interview, Ferrie emphatically denied he had been in Dallas on the day of the assassination. Yet no one in the FBI or Secret Service made much of an effort to verify exactly where Ferrie was that day. Ferrie insisted he was in Federal Court, attending Carlos Marcello's trial, but no one attempted to prove or disprove his statement. Would Marcello have been a good corroborating witness for Ferrie? Would the government have accepted his testimony as truthful after charging him with perjury on another matter?

Continuing to quote from the Secret Service report:

As the interview with David William Ferrie was about to end he stated that he had a very good idea who had reported him as having associated with Oswald, training him in the use of telescopic lenses, etc.; that he was firmly convinced that one Jack S. Martin who resides at the corner of Esplanade Avenue and N. Prieur Street had made this false report against him. He stated that Martin makes a habit of hanging around the offices of various attorneys, Court rooms, etc., and is well known locally for furnishing false leads to law enforcement officers, attorneys, etc.

That was Ferrie's evaluation of the man who had ordained him a bishop in the Old Catholic Church of North America—a fellow cultist. Was Ferrie unusually perceptive, or was Jack S. Martin really telling the truth? The Secret Service, and the FBI as well, chose to believe Ferrie. So did Assistant District Attorney Kohlman of the Orleans Parish District Attorney's office.

Again I quote from the Secret Service report:

Subsequent to our interview with Ferrie on the night of 11-25-63 he was interviewed by FBI agents at the First District Police Station.

On 11-26-63 it was learned that the FBI agents had talked with Jack S. Martin, who admitted that he had been the informant with regard to David William Ferrie; that

Martin had admitted to FBI agents that the information he had furnished Assistant District Attorney Kohlman was a figment of his [Martin's] imagination and that he had made up the story after reading the newspapers and watching television; that he remembered Kohlman, a former newspaper reporter, had written an article or story about Ferrie a couple of years ago and that he had pieced the whole thing together in his mind and given it to Kohlman as facts.

That was the same Jack Martin who had originally asked for anonymity. Knowing Ferrie's close-knit connections with the most powerful man in organized crime in the Southeast, what other choice did Martin have? Is it simply coincidence that Martin turned informant at approximately the same time Robert Mulholland of NBC News said he heard FBI agents discussing Ferrie in Dallas? How was it that NBC cameraman Gene Barnes profiled Ferrie so accurately in his statement to the FBI? How could all these facts possibly match up by mere coincidence? Martin had to know something of value, but apparently he felt helpless when he was forced by the FBI and Secret Service to surface publicly.

Returning to the conclusion of the Secret Service report:

On the night of 11-29-63, SAIC Rice and reporting agent interviewed Jack S. Martin at length in his small run-down apartment located at 1311 N. Prieur Street, New Orleans, which he shares with his wife and 6-year-old son. Martin, who has every appearance of being an alcoholic, admitted during the interview that he suffers from "telephonitis" while drinking and that it was during one of his drinking sprees that he telephoned Assistant District Attorney Herman S. Kohlman and told him this fantastic story about David William Ferrie being involved with Lee Harvey Oswald. He said he had heard on television that Oswald had at one time been active in the Civil Air Patrol and had later heard that Ferrie had been his squadron commander.

Martin stated that Ferrie was well known to him; that he recalled having seen rifles in Ferrie's home and also recalled that Kohlman had written an article on Ferrie and that Ferrie had been a Marine and had been with the Civil Air Patrol. Martin stated that after turning all these thoughts over in his mind, he telephoned Herman S. Kohlman and told his story as though it was based on facts rather than on his own imagination.

Were Robert Mulholland and Gene Barnes of NBC News imagining what they heard about Ferrie in Dallas? Was it a figment of their imagination? Was Ferrie so well known in Dallas that his homosexual activities were common knowledge there? Barnes, in particular, was quite candid in detailing what he knew about Ferrie. On the other hand, once Martin's mask of anonymity had been torn off, he was terrified of Carlos Marcello. And with good reason, since informants are not looked upon kindly by organized crime.

Secret Service agents Gerrots and Rice concluded their report, "In view of the above, this phase of the investigation involving David William Ferrie will be considered closed."

The report, as was mentioned previously, was considered so insignificant that the Warren Commission did not include it among the thousands of exhibits that stuffed the twenty-six volumes to the point of sheer boredom.

Yet it is a fact that Ferrie's name figured in the investigation of the JFK assassination almost from the very beginning and that no major attempt was made by law-enforcement agencies to disprove the possibility that he had a relationship with Oswald.

If the FBI was mistaken about "Jim Braden," it most certainly could be wrong about David William Ferrie. For one thing is certain—both were Mafia men for all seasons, and their trails crisscrossed through the cartels of organized crime.

XI

THE LITTLE MAN

I only met Carlos Marcello once. The date was April 23, 1970, and at first glance he hardly appeared to be the tyrannical Mafia despot described in testimony before Congressional committees. "The Little Man," as he was known to his associates, had been subpoenaed to appear before a racket-busting Federal Grand Jury in Los Angeles, which was particularly interested in the theft of half a million dollars in negotiable securities from a local brokerage house in 1968. Marcello's appearance was something of a surprise, since most Mafia watchers were unaware that his tentacles stretched all the way from New Orleans to the West Coast.

From the onset Marcello balked at answering questions. Federal Prosecutor David Nissen, in a vain attempt to force Marcello to testify, told a United States District Judge in open court that he was specifically interested in Marcello's connections with two Louisiana contractors, D'Alton Smith and J. W. Lambert. Smith had expanded his base of operations to California and was an "advance man" for Marcello. Smith was known to travel in the same circles as the mysterious "Jim Braden." Apart from his role in the security thefts, Smith was also under investigation for setting up rock festivals in California under Marcello's sponsorship. Word had it that "The Little Man" and his friends were trying to muscle in on the territory of Nick Licata, the embattled Mafia boss in Los Angeles, who at that time was serving an indefinite jail sentence for refusing to testify before the same Federal Grand Jury that had subpoenaed Marcello.

During a recess, as Marcello strolled down the courthouse corridor, mumbling to himself, a newspaper reporter nudged me and said, "You know, there's been a lot of talk about that guy being involved in the Kennedy assassination." I acknowledged I had heard the same story somewhere along the line but that it was difficult for me to believe that "The Little Man" could have directed the machinations of a conspiracy of such monumental proportions. But the reporter told me, "Don't ever underestimate Carlos Marcello."

As it happened, I found myself in the restroom at the same time as Marcello, who had been warned by his attorney, Cecil Burglass, not to discuss anything with members of the working press in Los Angeles.

"You know," Marcello told me, "every time I get called before one of these Federal Grand Juries, I think I got to keep going to the bathroom, only when I go there, I can't go. It upsets my stomach. I don't know what it is."

I suggested to Marcello that he might be afflicted with colitis. "Is that what you call it?" Marcello asked. "I didn't know what it was, but I've got it pretty bad." Marcello added that he didn't like Los Angeles one bit. "It's not like New Orleans. You ought to see the courthouse we've got in New Orleans. It's really something." I told Marcello the next time I was in Jim Garrison's country, I'd look up the courthouse. That seemed to please him.

It was difficult to be impressed by "The Little Man" unless you read his press clippings in advance.

That day everywhere I looked in the courthouse I saw intelligence officers from various agencies: the FBI, the Criminal Conspiracy Unit of the LAPD, the Sheriff's office, and the California Justice Department. Several admitted to me that they just wanted to get a look at Marcello, a close-up view of the man considered the most powerful Mafia figure in the United States. One of the intelligence officers present that day was a friend of mine from the California Attorney General's office who knew all about "Jim Braden" and said that one of his goals in life was to see to it that Braden was put behind bars. The agent asked me to point Marcello out to him. I did, and he then walked up to the Mafia chieftain and handed him a subpoena, ordering Marcello to appear the next day in the office of the California Attorney General in Los Angeles. Attorney Cecil Burglass was outraged and started harping about the injustices he and his client had encountered in California. Burglass insisted he had been double-crossed, that he had been assured Marcello would be required to make only one appearance before a law-enforcement agency in southern California.

But there were a lot of questions for Marcello, even though he wouldn't answer any of them. It appeared to me that Marcello was being harassed deliberately, that state and federal officials, well aware of his power, were attempting to block him from setting up shop in southern California. There had been persistent reports that Marcello was interested in gaining control of the concessions aboard the British luxury liner *Queen Mary*, which was being turned into a convention center and tourist trap in nearby Long Beach.

After the Grand Jury hearing was over—with nothing apparently having been gained from Carlos Marcello—United States Attorney Matthew Byrne invited me into his office. Byrne's curiosity was aroused just as much by Marcello as mine was, and eventually the subject turned to David William Ferrie. I asked Byrne if he had heard the story about Ferrie flying Marcello back to the United States after Robert Kennedy had ordered "The Little Man" deported to Guatemala. I pointed out that Jim Garrison's associates in New Orleans insisted there was absolutely no truth to the story, that Marcello sneaked back into the United States aboard a shrimp boat.

"I don't care what Garrison or his friends say," Byrne snapped back at me. "I have an FBI report around here somewhere that says Ferrie was the one who flew Marcello back from Guatemala."

It was at that point that the Garrison investigation became suspect in my mind. Was it true that Ferrie was not just the right-wing extremist pictured by Garrison? What was Garrison up to in New Orleans?

I wasn't the only one to learn about that plane trip. Leaks about Marcello were becoming more and more common as members of the United States Justice Department under the new Attorney General, John Mitchell, started bearing down on "The Little Man" and his far-flung operations.

On September 4, 1970, Nicholas C. Chriss, a reporter for the *Los Angeles Times*, did a profile on Marcello from New Orleans. Chriss wrote:

In December, 1952, he [Marcello] was ordered deported but he successfully fought the order until April, 1961 when he was deported to Guatemala through the efforts of former Atty. Gen. Robert F. Kennedy. After Italy had refused to accept Marcello, he came up with a birth certificate in an obscure Guatemalan town. Within two months he had returned to Louisiana, flown there secretely by David Ferrie, who later figured in New Orleans Dist. Atty. Jim Garrison's investigation of an alleged conspiracy to kill President John F. Kennedy.

145

Ferrie, of course, had admitted making those trips to Guatemala to assist Marcello during "The Little Man's" perjury trial. The people around Jim Garrison are extremely defensive about the D.A.'s relationship with Marcello. They claim Marcello was "kidnapped" by Bobby Kennedy and that his acquittal at that perjury trial was a "smashing victory" for the forces of law and order.

The date was April 4, 1961, and Marcello was making his quarterly visit to the United States Immigration Office in New Orleans—as he was required to do by law, since his status was that of an immigrant—when suddenly two Justice Department agents rushed up to him, threw his arms behind his back and handcuffed him. Then they forced Marcello into a waiting black limousine, and drove him to the New Orleans Airport, where he was placed aboard a private jet and flown to his adopted homeland, Guatemala. Obviously Bobby Kennedy had no respect for the Mafia's royalty. During his two months' stay in the Central American republic, Marcello was wined and dined by a number of high-placed government officials who recognized him for what he was, the king of all he surveyed in Louisiana.

Following Marcello's return to the United States with Ferrie, Robert Kennedy announced plans for a federal prosecution. He said he would charge "The Little Man" with perjury on the grounds that Marcello had lied to Immigration Department officials when he said he was born in Guatemala. Two of those who collaborated in

Marcello's defense, as the record shows, were David Ferrie and Attorney G. Wray Gill. Those two trips Ferrie made to Guatemala in October of 1963 were intended to gain proof that Marcello had indeed been born in that country. Ferrie did his legal homework well, at least well enough to vindicate Marcello in his running battle with Bobby Kennedy.

On November 22, 1963, the day of the JFK assassination, a Federal Court jury in New Orleans acquitted Marcello of the charges brought against him by Robert Kennedy. David Ferrie insisted he was with Marcello when the verdict was returned —not in Dallas on another mission, as some had speculated.

Even prior to the trial, word started circulating that Marcello wanted revenge against the Kennedys for his unceremonious deportation. Mafia-watcher Ed Reid in his book *The Grim Reapers,* a study of la Cosa Nostra's membership across the United States, maintained that Marcello plotted to kill the Kennedy brothers and talked about using a "nut" to do the job. (What better "nut" than Lee Harvey Oswald and what better man to find him than David William Ferrie, who had an uncanny way of attracting young men into lurid homosexual relationships?)

Reid told me he obtained details of the alleged plot from an informant who was present at a meeting called by Marcello in September of 1962. According to Reid, the meeting took place at a country farmhouse outside New Orleans and was attended by Marcello's most trusted associates. The conversation turned to Attorney General Robert Kennedy, and the informant quoted Marcello as crying out: "Take the stone out of my shoe. Don't worry about that little Bobby sonofabitch. He's going to be taken care of."

The informant said that Marcello realized that to eliminate Bobby he would first have to take care of his brother, the President. He noted that Bobby was usually closeted in his office in Washington, while the President was much more accessible, constantly moving about the country. Hence John Kennedy would be a much easier mark. The informant said there was no doubting that Marcello was serious and that he considered his deportation worthy of a "Sicilian vendetta."

It was about the same time that Robert Kennedy was making plans for a massive war on organized crime, with special emphasis on Mafia activity in Las Vegas and the southeastern United States. Bickering and animosity had developed between the Attorney General and FBI Director J. Edgar Hoover because of Kennedy's contention that Hoover focused too much of the bureau's attention on the Communist Party and neglected the inroads being made in financial circles by the organized underworld.

In the words of intelligence officers, members of the Mafia felt that Bobby Kennedy was "leaning hard" on them. Carlos Marcello knew from personal experience that Bobby Kennedy meant business, and he wanted to avoid a repetition of that flight to Guatemala.

It has almost become fashionable to view the Mafia with sympathy. Joseph Colombo could attract thousands to New York's Times Square with his Italian-American civil-rights movement.

Mafia-watcher Gay Talese, author of "Honor Thy Father"—a somewhat sympathetic profile of Joe Bonnano's oldest son, Bill—indicates that the Mafia has been more sinned against than sinning.

Writing in the *New York Times*, Talese had this to say about the Mafia:

> When the average American citizen thinks about the Mafia, he usually contemplates scenes of action and violence, of dramatic intrigue and million dollar schemes, of big black limousines screeching around corners with bullets spraying the sidewalk.
>
> This is the Hollywood version and it widely exaggerates reality; ignoring the dominant mood of Mafia existence: endless waiting, tedium and hiding, excessive smoking, overeating, lack of physical exercise, reclining in rooms behind drawn shades, being bored to death while trying to stay alive.
>
> With so much time and so little to do with it, the member of the Mafia tends to become self-consumed and self-absorbed, focusing on minutiae and magnifying them, overreacting to each sound, overinterpreting what is said and done, losing perspective of the larger

world beyond, and his very small place in the world, but nevertheless being aware of the exaggerated image that the world has of him; and he responds to it, believes it, prefers to believe it, for it makes him larger than he is, more powerful, more romantic, more respected and feared.

That is Gay Talese's version of the Mafia—one sadly out of touch with reality.

Carlos Marcello is a Mafia killer, despite the protestations of certain persons and groups who would glorify such contemporary killers in the same way certain writiers of Western stories eulogized Billy the Kid.

An article in the April 10, 1970, *Life* magazine reported that Louisiana's notorious "Little Man" was bigger than ever. Quoting directly from *Life*:

People who cross the Little Man still get killed. In 1967, for example, Harry Bennett, a Marcello syndicate gambler, was gunned down 13 hours after he was seen approaching a federal prosecutor with an offer to testify against the boss. Last fall Donald ("Jimmie") James, who had been Bennett's partner in a Gulf Coast gambling casino, also ran afoul of Marcello. James' sin was to swindle a Marcello gang member out of $10,000. When he learned of it, Marcello found James and got the money back. In January, James was found shot to death in almost the exact spot where Bennett had been killed two years earlier.

Apparently Gay Talese never got a chance to observe Marcello operate in the bayou country.

There were frequent demands in New Orleans that Marcello and his friends be investigated, but on each occasion that Jim Garrison took a Grand Jury in tow, the conclusion was always the same: there was no evidence of organized crime in Orleans Parish.

Quoting again from the August 10, 1970 edition of *Life*:

From 1965 through 1969, Garrison obtained just two convictions and five guilty pleas in police cases brought against Marcello's gangsters. He dismissed 84 cases, including 22 gambling charges, one for attempted murder, three for kidnaping and one for manslaughter. Garrison even managed to hush up the fact that last June a Marcello bagman, Vic Carona, died after suffering a heart attack during a political meeting held in Garrison's own home.

Garrison has, on occasion, demanded to know why reporters are so curious about his alleged ties to the Mafia when they should be trying to determine the truth of the JFK assassination and the motives of the CIA and the FBI. There is no doubt that Jim Garrison has gone out of his way to avoid a confrontation with Marcello and his Mafia empire. And in so doing, Garrison has allowed Marcello to become one of the richest and most powerful men in Louisiana.

Marcello has a far-flung empire in New Orleans valued in the millions of dollars. He is almost as rich as a Rockefeller and much more powerful in his home territory. In 1970 the *Wall Street Journal* did a detailed study of Marcello's financial holdings in a front-page story that identified him as "the undisputed patriarch of the Cosa Nostra in Louisiana and the nearby Gulf Coast area."

Among Marcello's holdings are the 101-unit Town and Country Motel in New Orleans (where Marcello was frequently visited by David Ferrie); Southern Tours, Inc., a sightseeing bus service; the Elmwood Plantation Restaurant; the Sho-Bar burlesque palace on Bourbon Street; the Holiday Motel in Jefferson Parish (not to be confused with the Holiday Inn chain); and numerous other motels, restaurants, and tourist attractions throughout Louisiana. Many of the businesses are in the names of Marcello's sons and brothers.

The *Wall Street Journal* noted:

Carlos ("The Little Man") Marcello is a short, pudgy 59-year-old Sicilian who has successfully resisted deportation, served time in federal prison for marijuana peddling and now is appealing a two-year conviction for assaulting an FBI agent. . . . But his notoriety hardly hampers him and his relatives and associates in playing a major role in business here [New Orleans], along with the syndicate's more traditional interests in illegal gambling, narcotics, prostitution and other lucrative trades.

A short distance outside New Orleans, Marcello owns 4,164 acres of land, valued at $16 million, but in 1970 it was assessed at only $8,000, demonstrating his power over local government officials.

According to Aaron Kohn, head of the New Orleans Crime Commission and a bitter enemy of Jim Garrison, it is possible for a tourist visiting the city to stay at a motel, have a drink at a bar, and take a sightseeing tour of the city, all through the courtesy of companies owned by Marcello and his associates in the Mafia.

In 1951 the late Senator Estes Kefauver of Tennessee described Marcello as "one of the worst criminals in the country." "The Little Man" was said to be the envy of other Mafia families because of his enormous wealth and his stranglehold on Louisiana politicians. Ralph Salerno, a consultant to the National Council on Crime and Delinquency and perhaps the foremost expert on organized crime in the United States, summed up Marcello's business operations in two words, "smooth" and "efficient."

While Carlos Marcello was building his financial empire on a mountain of vice and corruption, Jim Garrison winked and looked the other way. He accused local judges of coddling the underworld, but when the subject of Carlos Marcello was brought up, he turned a deaf ear on it. When the D.A. needed a ride home from the New Orleans Athletic Club, one of Marcello's lieutenants supplied "Big Jim" with a chauffeured limousine.

Some of the investigators who flocked to New Orleans after Garrison revealed he was investigating the JFK assassination were astonished to find that Big Jim kept company with Marcello and his sons.

In September of 1967 *Life* printed a series of sensational charges involving Marcello's links to Garrison and Teamsters Union President James R. Hoffa, who, like Marcello, was a bitter enemy of the Kennedy family, whom he blamed for his eventual imprisonment.

Life specifically accused Garrison and Louisiana Governor John J. McKeithen of allowing Marcello's hoodlum empire to flourish "with a remarkable degree of official tolerance."

Life accused the governor of looking the other way while Marcello attempted to free Jimmy Hoffa from a federal penitentiary by offering a $1 million bribe to the principal government witness against Hoffa, Baton Rouge Teamsters official Edward G. Partin. Hoffa had been sentenced to eight years in prison for jury tampering on the basis of Partin's testimony. According to *Life*, Marcello dangled the $1 million bribe in front of Partin in the hope he would recant his testimony.

The magazine alleged the meeting was held in the home of Aubrey Young, a key assistant and confidant of Governor McKeithen.

The Governor, in turn, accused *Life* of a "deliberate smear" on Louisiana.

Life also charged that, during Garrison's investigation into the JFK assassination, the D.A. was the guest of one of Marcello's top lieutenants, Mario Marino, at the Sands Hotel, in Las Vegas.

According to the September 29, 1967, edition of *Life*:

> On August 16 Garrison freely admitted to two *Life* reporters that he had accepted Marino's hospitality—several hundred dollars worth—and he even produced a copy of one paid-in-full bill. But he denied seeing anything wrong with this. He also denied knowing that Marino had any connection with Marcello—or that it made any difference. "I don't have to worry about things like that," he said. "I've cleaned up the rackets in this town."
>
> Since the publication of *Life*'s [earlier] articles, Garrison has altered his view substantially in statements to New Orleans newspapers. "I have never been a guest of mobsters anywhere in my life," he now says. Then he adds, "My record speaks for itself and it should be obvious that mobsters and organized crime have no friend in me."

155

It took President Richard Nixon's Attorney General, John Mitchell, to break the truth to the American public, which at one time was inclined to believe in Jim Garrison.

On June 30, 1971, Mitchell announced that Garrison had been arrested on a federal complaint, charged with taking payoffs from underworld figures to protect illegal gambling traffic in pinball machines. It wasn't anything new. Pershing Gervais, once Garrison's chief investigator, was identified as the informant who exposed the corruption in Garrison's office. Gervais was quoted as saying that for nine years he had been the "conduit" for bimonthly payoffs to Garrison ranging from $2,000 to $3,000.

This is the same Jim Garrison who announced he had "solved" the assassination of President John Fitzgerald Kennedy, a man who kept company with some of the most notorious Mafia figures in the United States.

Garrison offered to resign if anyone could prove the charges made by *Life* were true. But when the United States Justice Department started proving them, Garrison charged that he was being framed because of his investigation into the JFK assassination. Carlos Marcello had no comment.

XII

THE PROXIMITY FACTOR

Eugene Hale Brading was no stranger to New Orleans. Federal parole records show he began traveling frequently to Louisiana in August of 1961. Once he was warned about making unauthorized trips there with Victor Pereira. On more than one occasion he advised parole officials in Los Angeles that he had business dealings in Louisiana with Roger Bauman. Most of the time Brading gave his destination as Lafayette, about 165 miles west of New Orleans. He maintained a bank account at the Hub City Bank of Lafayette, in addition to an account at the Bank of America branch in Oceanside, California, about one hundred miles south of Los Angeles.

Normally Brading advised parole officials that he would travel by commercial airliner to New Orleans, then by some other means of transportation to Lafayette.

The parole records show that Brading made several trips to New Orleans in the fall of 1963. But that does not necessarily mean that he saw David William Ferrie. Ferrie, of course, was also making airline trips in the fall of 1963, two of them to Guatemala on behalf of Carlos Marcello.

However, there is one crucial bit of evidence that does provide a proximity factor. David Ferrie worked out of Room 1707 in the Père Marquette Building, in New Orleans—the office of Marcello's attorney, G. Wray Gill. A check of federal records and correspondence showed that in addition to his office in Beverly Hills, California, Brading also shared office space on occasion in the Père Marquette Building, a few doors away from Ferrie in Room 1701. Is this just one more coincidence?

Room 1701 was the office of an oil geologist, Vernon Main, Jr. Brading received mail at that address, and at one time notified parole authorities that he would be working out of Main's office while he was in New Orleans. For some reason, Brading informed the parole authorities that he could be found in Room 1706 of the Père Marquette Building, which would have placed him right next door to David Ferrie. However, a check determined that Room 1706 had been occupied by the Pinkerton Detective Agency for many years, and 1701 was actually the room used by Brading. It appears likely that Ferrie and Brading were within shouting distance of each other in October of 1963. The parallels between the two cannot be ignored. Both were connected with the highest echelons of organized crime, Ferrie with Carlos Marcello in New Orleans, and Brading with members of the Mafia in both California and Colorado.

While Brading told his parole officer most of his business was in Lafayette, there is every reason to believe he spent considerable time in New Orleans.

With this in mind, recall the desperate effort Jim Garrison made to place Edgar Eugene Bradley in New Orleans prior to the assassination and in Dallas the day John Kennedy was murdered.

Gene Brading was in both cities during periods Garrison described as crucial to his investigation. Garrison maintained that Gene Bradley traveled to New Orleans "sometime" in September of 1963 to take part in the conspiracy. There is not one shred of proof that Bradley was in New Orleans during that period.

Garrison claimed Bradley was in Dallas the day of the JFK assassination, once again without proof. But Gene Brading was most definitely in Dallas—specifically, in Dealey Plaza, where he was taken into custody under the name of Jim Braden.

Garrison claimed that the three principals in the conspiracy were David Ferrie, Clay Shaw, and Gene Bradley. There is no evidence to support the D.A.'s contention that Bradley knew Ferrie, much less Clay Shaw. But there is a body of evidence that suggests that Gene Brading had every opportunity to encounter David Ferrie, not only because they both came out of the milieu of the Mafia, but because of the proximity factor in the Père Marquette Building in New Orleans.

Both Brading and Ferrie claimed they went to

Houston, Texas, the night of November 22, 1963; Brading after being released from custody by the Dallas County Sheriff's Office, Ferrie after standing by the side of Carlos Marcello at the Mafia chieftain's Federal Court perjury trial in New Orleans.

One must wonder about Jim Garrison's motives for indicting Edgar Eugene Bradley in light of the D.A.'s extremely questionable background—his relationship with Carlos Marcello and others involved in organized crime. High intelligence officers told me they were convinced that Garrison knew all about Eugene Hale Brading prior to the launching of his "investigation" in New Orleans. What the FBI did not know was that the "Jim Braden" arrested in Dealey Plaza was in reality Eugene Hale Brading.

The fact that Garrison was able to pluck Gene Bradley out of the millions of people in California and have Deputy Sheriff Roger Craig identify him as the mystery man in Dealey Plaza, seemed to be more than just a stroke of fate. Jim Garrison had almost pulled off his gigantic hoax in New Orleans and eliminated the last vestiges of belief in the Warren Commission's finding that Lee Harvey Oswald was a solitary killer. All the while, Garrison was being courted by the Mafia, taking their payoffs and proclaiming himself as the man who had solved the crime of the century.

The only official attempt to silence Garrison was made by Attorney General Ramsey Clark, and it was feeble, at best. Robert Kennedy had many misgivings about the Warren report, and he was well acquainted with Garrison's track record in New Orleans. But he did not speak out, and a year later he too was dead at the hands of an assassin.

Despite Garrison's malicious slander of Gene Bradley, there was virtually no one who would come to Bradley's aid. Gene Bradley walked a trail of doubt and torment; Gene Brading walked away from it all.

One of the best detectives I know once told me, "There is a logical explanation for everything in this type of work. Sometimes we simply miss the logic."

Logically, Gene Bradley could not have been involved in a conspiracy to murder President John Kennedy. Yet Jim Garrison was not being illogical. Perhaps he was using false logic to achieve his ends, but in all probability he was merely being devious.

Once again I must revert to the findings of the Warren Commission to bear out this contention. The men who framed those findings admitted that one question was left unanswered when they concluded that Lee Harvey Oswald acted alone. That unanswered question may in itself have been the answer to the enigmatic actions of Jim Garrison in New Orleans.

XIII

THE VOICE FROM THE PAST

One of those who volunteered his services to help Jim Garrison to implicate Edgar Eugene Bradley in the JFK assassination was Loran Eugene Hall, a swarthy bartender from Kernville, California, a soldier of fortune with a record of involvement in radical right-wing causes.

His niche in history can be found in the pages of the Warren report, for Loran Eugene Hall was another enigma—one apparently too difficult for the FBI to solve. At issue was whether Lee Harvey Oswald was a traveling companion of Loran Eugene Hall sometime in September of 1963.

Mrs. Sylvia Odio was born in Havana in 1937. She was a well-educated member of the upper class in Cuba. In 1960 she fled to the United States. According to the Warren Commission: "It appears that both her parents are political prisoners of the Castro regime. Mrs. Odio is a member of the Cuban Revolutionary Junta (JURE), an anti-Castro organization."

Sylvia Odio told the Warren Commission that

sometime in the fall of 1963 three men came to her apartment in Dallas to find out if she was "working in the underground." Mrs. Odio said she told the trio she was not a member of the anti-Castro underground.

Quoting directly from the Warren Commission's report:

She [Mrs. Odio] testified that two of the men appeared to be Cubans, although they had some characteristics she associated with Mexicans. These two men did not state their full names, but identified themselves only by their fictitious underground "war names." Mrs. Odio remembered the name of one of the Cubans as "Leopoldo."

The third man, an American, allegedly was introduced to Mrs. Odio as "Leon Oswald," and she was told that he was very much interested in the Cuban cause. Mrs. Odio said that the men told her that they had just come from New Orleans and that they were about to leave on a trip. Mrs. Odio testified that the next day Leopoldo called her on the telephone and told her it was his idea to introduce the American into the underground "because he is great, he is kind of nuts." Leopoldo also said that the American had been in the Marine Corps and was an excellent shot, and that the American said the Cubans "don't have any guts . . . because President Kennedy should have been assassinated after the Bay of Pigs and some Cubans should have done that, because he was the one who was holding the freedom of Cuba actually.

Sylvia Odio testified that the three men visited her apartment prior to October 1, 1963, probably on September 26 or 27. She positively identified the American visitor as Lee Harvey Oswald and the Cuban "Leopoldo" as Loran Eugene Hall.

Edward Jay Epstein, one of the first critics of the Warren Commission, expressed considerable interest in Mrs. Odio's story and tried to pursue it. But he soon discovered he was chasing straws in the wind.

Epstein had originally written the story of the Warren Commission investigation as a thesis for his Master's degree. Commission investigators went along with his scholarly pursuits, not realizing that he would turn his thesis into a best-selling book entitled *Inquest*.

He recalled that when a Warren Commission lawyer once suggested that Sylvia Odio's story be checked out in greater detail, an unnamed superior advised the counsel, "At this stage we are supposed to be closing doors, not opening them."

If that was the official attitude, what chance did the American people have of learning the truth? It is obvious that the Warren Commission's investigation was sloppy. And there was at least a hint of suppression in the failure to include the investigation of David Ferrie anywhere in the twenty-six volumes of the Warren report. But on the matter of Sylvia Odio, the Commission was downright devious.

The Commission did not even conclude the investigation of Sylvia Odio's story. When the Warren report was issued, the matter of her testimony was still unresolved, and the American people were given this explanation:

In spite of the fact that it appeared almost certain that Oswald could not have been in Dallas at the time Mrs. Odio says he was, the Commission requested the FBI to conduct further investigation to determine the validity of Mrs. Odio's testimony. On September 16, 1964, the FBI located Loran Eugene Hall in Johnsandale, California. Hall had been identified as a participant in numerous anti-Castro activities. He told the FBI that in September of 1963 he was in Dallas, soliciting aid in connection with anti-Castro activities. He was accompanied by Lawrence Howard, a Mexican-American from East Los Angeles, and one William Seymour from Arizona. He stated that Seymour is similar in appearance to Lee Harvey Oswald; he speaks only a few words of Spanish as Mrs. Odio testified one of the men who visited her did. While the FBI has not yet completed its investigation into this matter at the time the report went to press, the commission has concluded that Lee Harvey Oswald was not at Mrs. Odio's apartment in September of 1963.

That is how the Warren Commission closed the door on what was probably its most significant testimony in 1964. Like Deputy Sheriff Roger Craig, Sylvia Odio may have seen something the Warren Commission did not want her to see. The framers of the Warren report considered Mrs. Odio's testimony in this light:

Although Mrs. Odio suggested doubts that the men were in fact members of JURE, she was certain that the American who was introduced to her as Leon Oswald was Lee Harvey Oswald. Her sister, who was in the apartment at the time of the visit by the three men, and who stated that she saw them briefly in the hallway when answering the door, also believed that the American was Lee Harvey Oswald. By referring to the date on which she moved from her former apartment, October 1, 1963, Mrs. Odio fixed the date of the alleged visit on the Thursday or Friday immediately preceding that date, i.e., September 26 or 27. She was positive that the visit occurred prior to October 1.

During the period of its investigation, however, the Commission concluded that Oswald could not have been in Dallas on September 26 or 27, 1963. It also developed considerable evidence that he was not in Dallas at any time between the beginning of September and October 3, 1963. On April 24, Oswald left Dallas for New Orleans, where he lived until his trip to Mexico City in late September and his subsequent return to Dallas.

Oswald is known to have been in New Orleans as late as September 23, 1963, the date on which Mrs. Paine and Marina Oswald left New Orleans for Dallas. Sometime between 4 P.M. on September 24 and 1 P.M. on September 25, Oswald cashed an unemployment compensation check at a store in New Orleans; under normal procedures this check would not have reached Oswald's postal box in New Orleans until at least 5 A.M. on September 25. The store at which he cashed the check did not open until 8 A.M. Therefore, it appeared that Oswald's presence in New Orleans until sometime between 8 A.M. and 1 P.M. on September 25 was quite firmly established.

But does that mean that Oswald could not have been in Dallas that same evening, in this age of modern transportation? One might presume the Warren Commission guilty of "horse and buggy" thinking.

Although there is no firm evidence of the means by which Oswald traveled from New Orleans to Houston, on the first leg of his

Mexico City trip, the Commission noted that a Continental Trailways bus leaving New Orleans at 12:30 P.M. would have brought Oswald to Houston at 10:50 P.M. that evening. His presence on the bus would be consistent with other evidence before the Commission.

At this point the Commission made a presumption, then virtually transformed it into evidence.

There is strong evidence that on September 26, 1963, Oswald traveled on Continental Airlines bus number 5133 which left Houston at 2:35 A.M. for Laredo, Tex. Bus company records disclose that one ticket from Houston to Laredo was sold during the night shift on September 25-26, and that such ticket was the only one of its kind sold in the period of September 24-26.

But does this satisfactorily explain the period from 1 P.M. on September 25—giving the Warren Commission the full benefit of the doubt—to the evening of that same day, when Mrs. Odio said she saw Oswald and three other men in New Orleans? There is not one shred of evidence to place Oswald on a bus that day. But there is evidence that places him in Dallas on the evening of September 25—the testimony of Mrs. Odio. Why should one presume that Oswald did all his traveling by bus?

The agent who sold this ticket has stated that Oswald *could* have been the purchaser. Two English passengers, Dr. and Mrs. John B. McFarland testified that they saw Oswald riding alone on the bus shortly after they awoke at 6 A.M. The bus was scheduled to arrive in Laredo at 1:20 P.M. on September 26, and Mexican immigration records show that Oswald in fact crossed the border at Laredo to Nuevo Laredo, Mexico, between 6 A.M. and 2 P.M. on that day. Evidence set out in appendix XIII established that Oswald did not leave Mexico until October 3, and that he arrived in Dallas the same day.

What, in the way of proof or evidence, has the Warren Commission offered so far to show that Oswald was not at Mrs. Odio's apartment on September 25?

The Commission noted that the only time not strictly accounted for during the period that Mrs. Odio thought Oswald might have visited her is the span between the morning of September 25 and 2:35 A.M. on September 26. The only public means of transportation by which Oswald could have traveled from New Orleans to Dallas in time to catch his bus from Houston to Laredo, would have been the airlines. Investigation disclosed no indication that he flew between these points.

What about Oswald's relationship with David Ferrie, which the Commission chose to ignore? Ferrie was a veteran pilot, and had flown his own plane in the fall of 1963. How easy would it have been for Ferrie to shuttle Oswald from New Orleans to Dallas? Ferrie had been seen a number of times at the New Orleans airport. But the Commission did not investigate his flight plans.

Moreover, it did not seem probable that Oswald would speed from New Orleans, spend a short time talking to Sylvia Odio, and then travel from Dallas to Mexico City and back on the bus. Automobile travel in the time available, though perhaps possible, would have been difficult. The Commission noted, however, that if Oswald had reached Dallas on the evening of September 25, he could have traveled by bus to Alice, Tex., and there caught the bus which had left Houston for Laredo at 2:35 A.M. on September 26, 1963. Further investigation in this regard indicated, however, that no tickets were sold between the period September 23-26, 1963 for travel from Dallas to Laredo or points beyond by the Dallas office of Continental Trailways, the only bus line on which Oswald could have made connections with the bus on which he was later seen. Furthermore, if Oswald had traveled from Dallas to Alice, he would not have reached the Houston to Laredo bus until after he was first reportedly observed on it by the McFarlands. Oswald had also told passengers on the bus to Laredo that he had traveled from New Orleans by bus, and made no mention of an intervening trip to Dallas.

If you were Oswald, would you have discussed any trip to Dallas at that point?

In addition, the Commission noted evidence that on the evening of September 25, 1963, Oswald made a telephone call to a party in Houston proposing to visit a resident of Houston that evening and the fact that such a call would appear to be inconsistent with Oswald's having been in Dallas at the time. It thus appeared that the evidence was persuasive that Oswald was not in Dallas on September 25, and therefore, he was not in that city at the time Mrs. Odio said she saw him.

The Warren Commission did not tell us where Oswald was calling from when he phoned that party in Houston. In an investigation of this magnitude, shouldn't that point have been crucial? Furthermore, the Warren Commission does not suggest that Oswald visited anyone in Houston on the evening of September 25.

Once again, there is nothing but speculation and conjecture on the part of the Commission when dealing with Sylvia Odio's story.

Furthermore, her testimony was corroborated by another witness, Evaristo Rodriguez, who had no connection with Mrs. Odio.

Excerpting again from the Warren Report:

The Commission also noted the testimony of Evaristo Rodriguez, a bartender in the Habana Bar in New Orleans, to the effect he saw Oswald in that bar in August of 1963 in the company of a Latin-appearing man. Rodriguez' description of the man accompanying the person he thought to be Oswald was similar in respects to the description given by Sylvia Odio since both testified that the man may have been of either Cuban or Mexican extraction, and had a slight bald spot on the forepart of his hairline. Rodriguez' identification of Oswald was uncorroborated except for the testimony of the owner of the bar, Orest Pena; according to Rodriguez, Pena was not in a position to observe the man he thought later to have been Oswald. Although Pena has testified that he did observe the same person as did Rodriguez, and that this person was Oswald, an FBI interview report indicated that a month earlier Pena had stated that he "could not at this time or any time say whether or not the person was identical with Lee Harvey Oswald." Though when testifying, Pena identified photographs of Oswald, the FBI report also recorded that Pena "stated that the only reason he was able to recognize Oswald was because he had seen Oswald's picture in the news media so often after the assassination of President John F. Kennedy." When present at Pena's bar, Oswald was supposed to have been intoxicated to the extent that he became ill, which is inconsistent with other evidence that Oswald did not drink alcoholic beverages to excess.

Once again the Warren Commission was looking for a loophole. Oswald didn't drink to excess, he didn't drive, and so on, ad infinitum.

The man who fit the verbal portrait painted by Sylvia Odio and Evaristo Rodriguez was Loran Eugene Hall. The FBI had gone so far as to track him down in California. He appeared to be of Latin descent despite his surname. He had a slight bald spot on the "forepart of his hairline." Furthermore, he admitted visiting Mrs. Odio in September of 1963. But the matter was dropped because the FBI had not concluded its investigation by the time the Warren Commission was ready to go to press.

My investigation revealed that Hall was another enigma out of the pages of the Warren Commission, in the mold of "Jim Braden" and David Ferrie. When Hall came forward in 1968 to implicate Edgar Eugene Bradley as a conspirator in the JFK assassination, there were few who recognized that he was the same person who had been examined subjectively by the Warren Commission and whose story was left unfinished.

Once again, I discovered, a principal in the JFK investigation was not exactly who he said he was.

XIV

ANOTHER ALIAS

After the publication of the Warren report, Loran Eugene Hall categorically retracted his story that he and two other men had been to Sylvia Odio's apartment in Dallas sometime in September of 1963. The two men Hall originally said had accompanied him to the Odio apartment, Lawrence Howard and William Seymour, steadfastly maintained they had never gone there in the first place.

Seymour, the man originally described by Hall as being similar in appearance to Oswald, had at one time been active in anti-Castro circles in Miami. Neither he nor Howard had known criminal records.

Sylvia Odio, although almost driven to the point of a nervous breakdown, refused to retract her story. She identified two of the three men who visited her as Lee Harvey Oswald and Loran Eugene Hall.

At this point in my investigation, which was indeed a lonely one, I had satisfied myself that

"Jim Braden" and David Ferrie were not all they were said to be. But somewhere in this puzzle there was another man. Who was Loran Eugene Hall? Why had he suddenly come forward—when Jim Garrison summoned him—to implicate Edgar Eugene Bradley in the alleged New Orleans conspiracy?

I checked the records of the California Attorney General and was astonished to learn that Hall was more commonly known as Lorenzo Pascillo. What's more, secret reports that apparently had not been made available to the FBI described Pascillo as a member of the paramilitary organization known as the Minutemen.

Knowing what the Warren Commission had stated about Hall and what Sylvia Odio had testified to, I immediately turned my thoughts to New Orleans and the Camp Street address Lee Harvey Oswald had used on his Fair Play for Cuba literature. That, of course, was the address of Guy Bannister, also supposed to be a Minuteman, and Jack Martin, the private detective who fingered David Ferrie immediately after the assassination. Both Bannister and Martin had been extremely active in anti-Castro activities, as had Loran Eugene Hall. Furthermore, Hall had been placed with Oswald in both Dallas and New Orleans by witnesses.

To add to this eerie picture, the California Attorney General had information indicating that Oswald might have been a member of the same paramilitary organization and not the dedicated Communist he was supposed to be.

Loran Eugene Hall was originally subpoenaed as a witness by Jim Garrison. The subpoena alleged that Hall had checked into the YMCA in Dallas sometime in October of 1963 and remained there until John Kennedy was assassinated. The subpoena said Hall "brought a weapon to Dallas shortly before the assassination and had been jailed briefly by Dallas police in October."

Garrison had maintained that Hall had conferred in Dallas with Jack Ruby and "other individuals believed to be involved in the assassination."

The D.A. further alleged that Hall had been in New Orleans and was acquainted with David Ferrie. Garrison announced he was subpoenaing Hall on December 26, 1967. When informed of the subpoena, Hall said, "You're kidding." He admitted that he had been in Dallas during the time noted on the subpoena and also that he had been active in the Free Cuba movement. But he denied that he was familiar with any of the persons implicated by Garrison in the assassination, including Edgar Eugene Bradley.

But on May 2, 1968, Hall called a news conference in Los Angeles and announced that he was willing to go to New Orleans and appear as a material witness for Jim Garrison. He said his memory had been "jogged."

This is how Jerry Cohen of the *Los Angeles Times* reported the story:

Loran Hall said Thursday that Edgar Eugene Bradley attended a meeting here in September, 1963, where the possibility of killing President Kennedy was discussed.

At the same meeting, Hall claimed, Bradley questioned him about "contacts" he had made as an anti-Castro activist in Dallas, New Orleans and Miami.

Bradley later branded Hall's assertations "lies," saying: "He very quickly changed his story. He sounds too well rehearsed on what to say. It's real strange he said he didn't know me, hadn't ever seen me, then all of a sudden remembered some meeting I know nothing about."

Bradley, 49, is the North Hollywood man accused last year by New Orleans Dist. Atty. Jim Garrison of conspiring to assassinate Kennedy. He faces an extradition hearing in Sacramento June 5. Bradley is the West Coast representative for radio evangelist Dr. Carl McIntyre.

Hall is the ex-Kernville bartender and one-time Castro prisoner Garrison unsuccessfully sought to subpoena as a witness earlier this this year. He said at that time he knew none of the men accused by Garrison of plotting the assassination, including Bradley.

But Hall was granted an audience Tuesday with Edwin Meese, Gov. Reagan's legal affairs secretary, and told Meese that his memory had been "jogged" about persons he had met at meetings before the assassination.

He told Meese that at many of the meetings at which he delivered anti-Castro talks in 1963 persons present talked about killing the President.

Thursday, he named Bradley as a man who had overheard at least one such discussion.

He emphasized at a press conference at the Press Club that he was not accusing Bradley himself of suggesting the President be murdered.

But he said that Bradley "stood right beside me and couldn't help but hear" when it was suggested "we ought to get an assassination team and go take care of Kennedy."

He said Bradley reacted to the remark "as if he'd heard it before" and that it was made after he, Hall, had delivered a speech in a residence at 233 S. Lafayette Park Place.

Hall said the residence, since torn down, was occupied by a man he identified as "C. C. Wheat."

Records show a G. Clinton Wheat owned the home in 1963.

FBI records show that a man known as Clinton G. Wheat, also as George Clinton, has a lengthy prison record and served time for murder in Louisiana in the 1940s.

It seemed somewhat odd that Hall tried to implicate Bradley in such a flimsy fashion. When

Garrison first subpoenaed Hall as a material witness, Hall did not mention Bradley. And now, suddenly, Loran Eugene Hall, also known as Lorenzo Pascillo, was singing a different tune. Why?

It appeared that Jim Garrison was out to get Gene Bradley no matter what the cost. What is most amazing is that Garrison was able to produce Hall without bringing the Sylvia Odio visit to the forefront.

Gene Bradley acknowledged that sometime in 1963 he attended a lecture on anti-Communism given by a former FBI agent in the Lafayette Park district of Los Angeles. "At that meeting," Bradley said, "they invited me to come back and give a talk myself, since I had given lectures on world politics. It seemed to me that was what I talked about."

Bradley said he returned to the house in Lafayette Park and delivered a speech "in either August or July of 1963." He insisted that he did not hear any talk relating to the assassination of John Kennedy.

Hall's statements about Bradley had a faint ring of truth for several reasons. Clinton Wheat, at whose home the meeting was held, was a known racist, apart from being a convicted killer. In 1954 he had led The Committee of One Million Caucasians to March on Washington.

Loran Hall said that during the meeting at Wheat's home he repeatedly heard anti-Negro and anti-Jewish statements in addition to the conversation about killing President Kennedy.

Gene Bradley was not exactly a shrinking violet in far-right circles, but neither was he a criminal. For many years Bradley had worked for radio evangelist Carl McIntyre, founder of the American Council of Christian Churches. Until the Reverend McIntyre was expelled from the organization, it had been accused of being anti-Catholic, anti-Jewish, and anti-Negro.

In 1959, while John Kennedy was campaigning for the presidency, the American Council of Christian Churches, under Reverend McIntyre's leadership, issued the following statement:

> To nominate a Roman Catholic would precipitate a religious conflict of major proportions. Such a conflict would seriously divide the United States in an hour when the unity and welfare of the nation is of paramount importance in our cold war struggle with Communism.

Since Gene Bradley espoused McIntyre's doctrine, he was particularly vulnerable from Jim Garrison's standpoint. The New Orleans D.A. would have us believe that Loran Hall was simply a corroborating witness.

What about Loran Eugene Hall, also known as Lorenzo Pascillo? His criminal record showed that he had been arrested for writing bad checks in 1956 in Wichita, Kansas. In 1959 he was jailed by the Castro regime in Havana for "plotting revolutionary activities." Also in 1959, it must be noted, Jack Ruby traveled to Havana as a guest of a professional gambler, Lewis J. McWillie, on what was described as a purely social trip. It was reported that McWillie was briefly imprisoned in Havana at the same time as Hall. The Warren Commission noted that McWillie "left Cuba with strong feelings of hostility to the Castro regime."

In 1961, Hall was arrested once more in Wichita, this time for shoplifting. After that he set up a base of operations in California, from which he frequently traveled to Louisiana, Florida, and Texas, presumably involving himself in the anti-Castro movement.

Investigators for the California Department of Justice discovered his ties to the Minutemen after finding his name on a slip of paper following a meeting of the paramilitary group in the Los Angeles area. He was known to his fellow Minutemen as Lorenzo Pascillo. In fact, Carol Aydelotte, the North Hollywood woman who gave Gene Bradley's picture to Jim Garrison, was shown a picture of Hall and identified him as Lorenzo Pascillo, an activist in the paramilitary movement.

In Dallas Sylvia Odio had identified the Latin-appearing man who called on her as "Leopoldo." But the FBI identified that man positively as Loran Eugene Hall, and it seems probable that Mrs. Odio could have mistaken Leopoldo for Lorenzo.

Loran Eugene Hall was just one more twist in the convoluted path, but finally some important questions about him had been at least partially answered.

XV

THE INCRIMINATING WITNESSES

The majority of Jim Garrison's "incriminating witnesses" against Edgar Eugene Bradley were paramilitarists—ultra-right-wing fanatics who played with guns and envisioned themselves as modern-day Paul Reveres, saving the United States from a Communist takeover. There was Loran Eugene Hall, a member of the Minutemen, himself under suspicion in the Warren report. There was Dennis Mower, also a member of the Minutemen, who had been linked to other assassination plots. There was Carol Aydelotte, who had supplied Garrison with the picture of Gene Bradley. Mrs. Aydelotte had strong links to both the Minutemen and the American Nazi Party. The New Orleans D.A. had turned up an unusual kettle of fish.

David Ferrie, of course, worked for the Mafia. But his links to paramilitary movements were well defined. Ferrie kept a small arsenal in his apartment. One of his closest friends, Jack Martin, was extremely active in the anti-Castro movement and was associated with attorney Guy Bannister, who was also linked to the Minutemen.

Lee Harvey Oswald, conversely, was described as a dedicated Marxist, a turncoat who had defected to the Soviet Union. But Oswald defected from Russia, too, when he found it not to his liking.

In New Orleans Oswald depicted himself as a member of the far left. He was virtually a one-man band trumping up enthusiasm for the Fair Play for Cuba Committee as he passed out pamphlets and debated on television. But was this an accurate profile of the man who killed John Kennedy? Why did Oswald use the Camp Street address on his Fair Play for Cuba literature, when all the while that was the headquarters of two ultra-right-wingers, Guy Bannister and Jack Martin? Did Oswald simply pick the address out of the blue, or did he have knowledge of the men behind the scenes there? The latter would appear to be a distinct possibility based on this investigation.

I was somewhat startled during a conversation with an official of the California Attorney General's office in 1968, when he said that information picked up by agents in the field indicated that Oswald was connected with far-right extremist groups following his return from the Soviet Union; he was not the sniveling little Communist everyone thought him to be.

The Attorney General's official pointed out that undercover officers had infiltrated the Minutemen and were startled to hear members of the gun-toting cadre heap praise on Oswald and embrace him as one of their own. For many months I was reluctant to consider this possibility; it just seemed too farfetched. Perhaps, like most other people, I had been brainwashed by the Warren Commission into accepting Oswald at face value. But then, one by one, members of the Minutemen began to surface in the Garrison investigation in New Orleans, and I decided to take a long hard look at the matter.

Shortly after the Kennedy assassination, leaders of the Minutemen sent a warning letter to every legitimate member of the organization. Strict secrecy surrounded the distribution of the letter. It was mailed in a blind envelope, with no return address. But one of the men on the mailing list just happened to be an undercover agent.

The letter started with the salutation: "Dear Patriot." It said, in part:

> The Minuteman organization is now the object of an intensive investigation. Apparently this is part of the announced plan of the Warren Commission to investigate "possible connections" between the radical right and the assassination of President Kennedy.
>
> All real patriots will recognize that such an implication is without foundation. If Robert Kennedy had spent as much time investigating the Communist-Socialist movement as he did worrying about the pro-American move-

ment, then his brother would probably still be alive.

This will not prevent the "conspiracy" (through the use of the controlled news media) from trying to give the impression that the right-wing is somehow to blame for John Kennedy's death.

This is an extremely serious situation.

Most of our members will already be familiar with the facts that Earl Warren has voted to favor the Communists in almost every case involving this nation's internal security that has come before the Supreme Court since he has been a member of that body. Most, too, will be aware that when Earl Warren first heard of Kennedy's death that he immediately issued a statement blaming the assassination on "right-wing" fanatics. In fact, this investigating committee was set up just three days after the Communist newspaper, The Worker, made a suggestion to that effect. The Worker also suggested that Earl Warren be made the head of a committee exactly as has occurred.

Nicholas Katzenbach who was in charge of the Federal Marshals at Oxford, Mississippi, has been named as chief investigator for the Warren Commission.

J. Lee Rankin, General Counsel for the Warren Commission, in a recent letter to Congressman Henry B. Gonzales (of Texas) stated: "I can assure you that any relationship between the Minutemen and the assassination of President Kennedy will be carefully explored."

Many (perhaps all) major FBI offices have received identical memos from Washington to investigate Minutemen activities in their areas.

Treasury agents are making a special effort to determine the existence of any automatic weapons that might be owned by members of this organization.

From several cities we have received reports of postal employees being assigned the special task of listing the names and addresses of persons who receive mail from the John Birch Society and other anti-Communist organizations.

There is considerable evidence to indicate that a nationwide propaganda campaign to blame President Kennedy's death on the right-wing had been organized before the assassination. If it had not been for the very good fortune that Oswald was quickly captured and identified as being a Communist, it is probable that hundreds of American patriots would be behind bars today.

We are now witnessing the gradual takeover of our government by hidden Communists to such an extent that loyal Americans are being subjected to "investigation," harassment and economic persecution.

THE TIME IS PAST WHEN THE COM-

MUNIST-SOCIALIST MOVEMENT CAN
BE SUCCESSFULLY OPPOSED BY ORGA-
NIZATIONS THAT OPERATE IN THE
OPEN. SUCCESSFUL OPPOSITION TO
THE COMMUNIST-SOCIALIST MOVE-
MENT NOW REQUIRES THE SECRET
METHODS OF A PATRIOTIC RESIS-
TANCE MOVEMENT.

We realize that many patriots will not give
up the hope of winning by political means
but we must remind our members again that
there are many people willing to work politi-
cally and only a few who will now begin to
build the final line of defense.

Although most individual agents of the
FBI are loyal Americans of the highest type,
we must constantly keep in mind that any
information they obtain about us will be
sitting in their files when the Communists
take over and will certainly be used against
us.

This paragraph was construed by intelligence
agents as a warning by the Minutemen not to
discuss the assassination with any member of law
enforcement—much less the FBI.

Continuing to quote from the letter:

If you are questioned as to whether or
not you are a member of this organization,
we advise you to deny it absolutely. Keep
your mind on the fact that they cannot prove

you are a member. Such information will NEVER be given out by the National or Regional headquarters. Our files are kept in such a manner that they cannot be seen under any circumstances.

If you are confronted with evidence indicating membership in the MM, say that you did inquire, have received literature from us, and possibly even subscribed to our newsletter simply because you are an open-minded person that likes to see both sides of every question, but you did not join.

In making contact with our members, we are faced with increasing costs due to the necessity of sending all mail first class, and from many different post offices. We need the continued financial support of every member if we are to operate in a secure and efficient manner.

Enclosed is a special sheet of practical suggestions regarding security measures which we recommend all members to follow.

Now is the time for each of us to determine whether or not we have the strength and courage of our forefathers. Are we made in the same mold as those Americans who pledged their lives, their fortunes, and their sacred honor to the cause of freedom?

Was this letter the result of paranoia, or did the Minutemen indeed have something to fear? Why should they go underground if they were satisfactorily convinced that Lee Harvey Oswald was a dedicated Marxist?

The Minutemen were nervous. A short time later an intelligence agent received another unsigned letter from the organization.

It said:

Ex-President Kennedy once said, "Right-wing extremists are a greater threat than the communists." It is too bad he couldn't have lived long enough to know who it was that shot him.

Immediately after his death a full propaganda campaign was immediately started to blame his death on these "right-wing extremists." Only the quick capture of Lee H. Oswald, a 24 year old dedicated communist put a temporary halt to this campaign. Even so, the news media of this country could hardly restrain themselves in their talk about "hate groups" and the "lunatic fringe." Our State Department immediately after Oswald was captured and identified contacted the major news services, TV networks etc., requesting them to "play down the possibility that Mr. Oswald was or is a communist."

Ironically enough, if Attorney General Robert F. Kennedy had kept current the list of subversive communist & socialist organizations and had enforced the Smith Act and the McCarren Act to clamp down on the hundreds of these organizations functioning in the United States, as he was supposed to, the death of his brother may have been averted.

Prior to the arrival of President Kennedy in Dallas, the city and State law enforcement agencies at the request of the Federal Government maintained close surveillance on anti-communist organizations and individuals, but they failed to check communist groups and individuals. Had they maintained an equally close check of left-wing extremists, the assassination may again have been averted. Two weeks before Kennedy was killed, the FBI questioned Oswald in Dallas about his trip to Mexico City where he contacted the Communist governments of Cuba and Russia. Shortly before this turn-coat ex-marine was arrested and found guilty for disturbing the peace when he was involved in a fight while distributing communist propaganda in the downtown area of a large city.

That Oswald was a communist is an absolute and proven fact. He was a subscriber to both the communist "Worker" and the socialist "Militant." He was (contrary to published reports) the official chairman of the New Orleans Chapter of the "Fair Play for Cuba." Oswald was in a position for quite some time to maintain close liaison with over 20 communist organizations throughout the United States. There is good reason to believe that Oswald had advance knowledge of the President's exact route of travel and that he came to Dallas and obtained a job at the book suppository [sic] overlooking this route, for the very specific purpose of performing the assassination.

Now that Oswald has been executed and his lips silenced forever, the campaign to blame this whole thing on the right-wing is rolling once again. Leaders of various patriotic movements are being systematically questioned by the FBI regarding their movements before, during and after the time of Kennedy's assassination. The National Coordinator of the Minutemen Organization was quizzed by the FBI in this regard at 11:00 A.M. November 29, 1963; the West Coast coordinator was "talked to" the afternoon of November 24th, 1963.

Again one must ask: was this simply paranoia or was there legitimate cause to suspect the Minutemen? Was there concern in the Minutemen's hierarchy about the health and welfare of Loran Eugene Hall?

Continuing to quote from the letter:

Although the district attorney office in Dallas stated that the evidence against Oswald was conclusive, others are not willing to let it go so easily. President Johnson has appointed Earl Warren (of all people) to head a "Board of Inquiry" to re-hash this investigation. Warren's appointment to head such a board was first suggested by the COMMUNIST PARTY OF AMERICA three days before it was ever known who was on the board. Now it has been announced that the FBI reports which were going to be made public, will not be, but only that information which this board deems the American public should know. . . . It would not surprise us a bit if this Board of Inquiry "discovers" that Oswald was not actually the assassin, but that he was a right-winger in disguise or something else equally fantastic.

It appears at this point that the Minutemen protest too much. The Warren Commission, of course, never considered the possibility that Oswald was a right-winger, nor did the investigators consider the possibility that he might be connected with Guy Bannister, Jack Martin and others who flocked to the Camp Street address in New Orleans—the same address used by Oswald on his literature. The possibility that Oswald might have traveled in the company of Loran Eugene Hall was dismissed, even though the FBI had not completed its investigation by the time the Warren report went to press, and though a body of evidence strongly suggested that the President's assassin traveled with a member of the Minutemen.

The letter concluded:

WHY WAS KENNEDY KILLED? The thing that mystified most American patriots is why the communists would want Kennedy dead. It would require pages and pages to list all of the things which Kennedy did while in office that directly aided the Communist cause.

There are several possibilities: (1) It is possible that Oswald was simply carried away with his own propaganda. (2) Like Stalin, Beria and others, Kennedy may have simply outlived his usefulness. (3) His assassination could have simply been a by-product of a known plot (or should we say a very well known plot) to set up a coalition government in Cuba timed to re-assure Kennedy's re-election in 1964. (4) It may have been part of the current conflict between the Stalinist and Trotskyite branches of the communist party, such as with the assassination of Trotsky in Mexico. The reasoning and evidence behind these possibilities will be dealt with in our January issue of On Target.

Regardless of the reason for his assassination the results are becoming quickly evident. (1) Congress is being pressured into rushing through the Kennedy programs in tribute to him. (2) By far the biggest and most extensive drive yet in American history to outlaw firearms of all types is quickly going into high gear on the state and national level.

The letters are important in that they tune us in to the thinking of the Minutemen, their theories and beliefs. Many law-enforcement officials have tended to regard the Minutemen as freaks, misguided superpatriots who play with guns and rifles but seldom do any harm.

But one cannot easily overlook the fact that the Minutemen supplied Jim Garrison with the bulk of his incriminating testimony against Edgar Eugene Bradley, the look-alike for "Jim Braden" in Dealey Plaza. Perhaps this was a direct spin-off of Loran Eugene Hall's travels with Lee Harvey Oswald, if one accepts the possibility that they were indeed traveling together.

The Minutemen are a strange but clever breed of revolutionary. Their importance cannot be underestimated in this investigation.

XVI

MINUTEMEN IN ACTION

On July 12, 1969, after a manhunt that lasted nearly nineteen months, the national leader of the Minutemen, Robert Bolivar de Pugh, was seized by FBI agents at his hideout in Truth or Consequences, New Mexico, along with his number-one aide, William Patrick Payson. They were charged with conspiring to rob a string of banks in the state of Washington in January of 1968 in order to finance "the last line of defense against Communism."

The philosophy expounded in those two previously quoted letters to rank-and-file members of the organization was the philosophy of Robert Bolivar de Pugh, zealot extraordinary.

During World War II de Pugh had been a United States Army radar engineer. He lived in Independence, Missouri, the hometown of former President Harry Truman. Soon after the war de Pugh became convinced that the United States was headed for a Communist takeover, and when John Kennedy became President, his worst fears seemed realized. Robert de Pugh took to the road, meeting with members of his secret organization across the United States and planning a plethora of bombings and assassinations. John Kennedy was singled out for assassination time and time again at meetings of the clandestine paramilitary movement.

Robert de Pugh was a revolutionary on the run. He had been sentenced to one year in prison in January of 1968 for transporting a pistol from Des Moines, Iowa, to Kansas City, Missouri, while under indictment in Jackson County, Missouri, on charges of possessing bombs and bombshells. De Pugh jumped bail, and bank robberies in the Seattle area quickly followed.

When de Pugh and Payson were arrested, they were heavily armed, according to the FBI, but did not offer any resistance. Information obtained by the bureau indicated that the two Minutemen leaders were in the throes of planning a "violent revolution."

De Pugh's prime mover on the West Coast was Dennis Mower, the young man who had come forward to link Edgar Eugene Bradley to several plots to kill John Kennedy. His allegiance to de Pugh was a matter of public record. In 1967, at the age of twenty-one, Mower was convicted by a Federal Court jury in St. Louis, Missouri, of transporting a stolen machine gun from Santa Ana, California, to Independence, Missouri, at that time the main headquarters of the Minutemen movement. During the trial Mower described himself as a "former Minuteman." He said he no longer engaged in gun-running and instead was devoting all his energies to his work as an ordained minister of the gospel. The court gave Mower a suspended two-year prison sentence.

Mower had indeed been ordained a minister in the Church of Jesus Christ Christian by the Reverend Wesley Swift, perhaps one of the most notorious right-wing extremists in California. Swift is credited with founding a paramilitary movement known as the California Rangers; he was also involved in the California League Against Communism, the Anglo-Saxon Christian Congregation, and the Christian Defense League. He was also identified by the California Attorney General as a Ku Klux Klan organizer in the Antelope Valley, about forty miles north of Los Angeles, and also as a "former KKK rifle team instructor."

Mower maintained his ministry at a church in the Lancaster area in the Antelope Valley. State investigators said that the primary purpose of Mower's church was to screen prospective members of the Minutemen. Although the Reverend Swift presided at a church in Los Angeles, his home was in Lancaster (near Mower's church). In Swift's back yard there was a rifle range for use by those recruited into paramilitary service.

Despite Mower's insistence that he had severed his ties with the Minutemen, as he claimed when he appeared in United States District Court in St. Louis in 1967, he continued to guide the activities of the organization in Southern California and offered his advice to other chapters across the country.

In 1968 investigators pinpointed Mower as the prime suspect in the dynamiting of the San Fernando Valley Peace Center, operated by pacifists opposed to the war in Vietnam. No one was killed in the blast, but the building was demolished. It was finally determined that there was insufficient evidence to prosecute Mower, the main problem being a lack of witnesses.

Later that same year, on June 30, 1968, Mower was linked to a plot to assassinate Jewish community leader Meyer Davidson in Meridian, Mississippi. Law-enforcement officers in Meridian had been repeatedly frustrated in their attempts to solve seventeen bombings and burnings that had terrorized the Negro and Jewish communities in that city. Most of the nightrider attacks were carried out against homes, churches, and the local synagogue. Finally the FBI was asked for assistance, and a trap was set with the help of three informants—two of them Klansmen —who were paid a total of $36,500.

When Albert Tarrants, III, and a pretty young school teacher, Mrs. Kathy Ainsworth, arrived at the Meyer Davidson home to carry out the planned assassination, they were trapped in a violent gun battle with officers of the Mississippi Highway Patrol. Mrs. Ainsworth was killed, and Tarrants, a policeman, and a bystander were wounded.

Evidence subsequently uncovered indicated

that Tarrants and Mrs. Ainsworth had been lured into the bombing attempt by the two Klansman who had received money from the FBI.

The policemen who sprang the trap said that they had anticipated a gun battle; they had never expected to take any Klan member alive. They had thought that the bombing would be carried out by two men and were surprised that a woman was involved. Gunfire broke out after Tarrants stepped out of his car, a pistol in one hand, dynamite in the other.

The conclusion was that the Klansmen who turned informants were well aware that Tarrants and Mrs. Ainsworth had carried out a number of bombings and decided to sell them out.

Roy Gunn, the Meridian Chief of Police, found a notebook in Tarrants' clothes which contained the following handwritten statement: "I have committed myself totally to defeating the Communist-Jew conspiracy—and all means necessary shall be used."

In addition to the notebook, the Chief of Police found the Reverend Dennis Mower's calling card among the items in Tarrants' possession. The card stated that Mower represented the "Southern California Freedoms Council," a more refined way of saying Minutemen, in the opinion of California intelligence officers. Beneath the title inscription were the words: *The Wages of Sin is* [sic] *Death.*

Subsequent investigation by California authorities determined that Tarrants had been in the Los

Angeles area several weeks prior to the attempted dynamiting of Meyer Davidson's home in Meridian, Mississippi, and had conferred secretly with Mower. The web was indeed a curious one. Why did Tarrants have to travel all the way to California to confer with a Minuteman? Perhaps it was because Dennis Mower was a past master of the art of dynamiting and could always supply the firepower, if needed.

Mower was never publicly implicated in the plot to murder Meyer Davidson. Tarrants received a thirty-year prison sentence, but eventually escaped from the Mississippi State Penitentiary in 1970.

Violence and intrigue had been a way of life for Dennis Mower since he was a teenager. In 1965, at the age of nineteen, he was implicated in a plot to smear Thomas Kuchel, at that time a Republican United States Senator from California, as a homosexual. According to a Los Angeles County Grand Jury transcript, Mower tried to confront Kuchel in his office at the United States courthouse in Los Angeles with an affidavit linking the liberal Senator to Walter Jenkins, the aide to President Johnson who resigned in disgrace after his homosexual activities became public knowledge.

At the time of the incident, Mower represented himself as the president of the Southern California Freedoms Council.

Los Angeles County District Attorney Evelle Younger (who later became the Attorney General of California) decided to prosecute those involved in the Kuchel smear, but Mower was granted immunity from prosecution in return for his testimony before the Grand Jury. The others implicated in the plot—one of whom was a Los Angeles policeman—were found guilty of criminal libel, perhaps the least-enforced statute in the California penal code.

Dennis Mower professed violence, and he spoke the language of bigots, more often than not taking his cue from the likes of Adolph Hitler.

Once, testifying at a California legislative hearing on a bill to ban genocide, Mower angrily declared, "My God was murdered by a minority group—the Jews."

The late newspaper columnist Paul Coates noted that Mower was extremely articulate and bright, and possessed unusual leadership qualities. But Coates predicted that Mower was headed in a direction that would make him a force for evil.

According to California intelligence agents who infiltrated meetings of the Minutemen presided over by Dennis Mower in the early 1960s, the rhetoric more often than not dealt with assassinating the "three Ks"—John Kennedy, Robert Kennedy, and Dr. Martin Luther King, Jr.—all of whom met violent deaths.

But was it just that, mere rhetoric? The public record shows it was not.

In February of 1965 Keith Gilbert, a ranking member of the Minutemen and one of Mower's closest associates, was accused by the Los Angeles police of masterminding a plot to kill Dr. King. Police charged that Gilbert planned to assassinate King by blowing up the Hollywood Palladium when the civil-rights leader spoke there. As proof, they offered 1,400 pounds of dynamite, which had been seized in a raid on Gilbert's apartment. While free on bond and awaiting trial, Gilbert fled to Canada. At first he had no visible means of support, but after a few weeks he began receiving checks for fairly substantial amounts from an unknown benefactor in the United States. Eventually, Gilbert was extradited to the United States by Canadian authorities and returned to Los Angeles, where he was found guilty of possessing explosives and was sentenced to a term of one to ten years in state prison.

While confined in San Quentin, the would-be assassin of Dr. King was interviewed on a number of occasions by intelligence officers from various law-enforcement agencies. Gilbert repeatedly indicated he had "something important" to discuss, but once the interviews began, he was evasive, usually moaning about how unpleasant it was to be in San Quentin.

Even though Gilbert was behind prison bars, he continued to receive checks for fairly substantial amounts from "benefactors" on the outside. One investigator referred to the checks as "hush money." Gilbert, however, insisted the checks were sent by persons who owed him considerable amounts of money. It was determined that some of the checks came from the Reverend Dennis Mower, who was not known to dabble in charity or lost causes.

Ironically, Gilbert's name was mentioned prominently during the investigation into the assassination of Senator Robert Kennedy in Los Angeles. Details of that investigation will be discussed in a subsequent chapter.

Keith Gilbert was indicative of a pattern set by Robert de Pugh's Missouri Minutemen. He was assigned to kill Dr. King. But there were other plots.

Several years after John Kennedy was murdered, FBI agents in Los Angeles launched a manhunt for a person identified as a "very dangerous right-wing extremist." Agents had obtained information that this man was hell-bent on killing a prominent political leader and in all probability was connected with the Missouri Minutemen.

Acting on a tip, FBI agents raced to a small cabin in the San Fernando Valley section of Los Angeles, where they arrested young Philip Earl Scheib, whom they found with a machine gun at his side. Scheib, of course, was the son of car-painter Earl Scheib, a prominent member of the Brading-Pereira axis. Was this just one more in a long line of curious coincidences?

Furthermore, young Scheib was a close associate of Dennis Mower. He was a ranking member of both the Minutemen and the American Nazi Party, which caused considerable trauma to his

Jewish parents, who nevertheless stood solidly behind him following his arrest.

FBI agents refused to talk about the assassination plot, or divulge exactly who was marked for assassination. But there was a flaw in the case that may account for the Bureau's silence. FBI agents summoned United States Treasury agents to the San Fernando Valley cabin to arrest Scheib, since possession of a machine gun is a crime that comes under the jurisdiction of the T-men. Scheib, with the best legal help his family could muster, escaped prosecution when a United States District Judge ruled that his Constitutional rights had beeen violated by an illegal search and seizure.

Quite obviously, Loran Eugene Hall, Dennis Mower, Keith Gilbert, and Philip Earl Scheib were not just ordinary paramilitarists who went out for target practice on Saturday afternoons. They took their cues from Robert de Pugh, a fanatic of the first order.

It was against this background, with this cast of characters, that Jim Garrison hoped to make a case against Edgar Eugene Bradley. But somehow, Garrison's cudgel had a hollow ring to it, which many recognized but few could understand.

Another principal in the Garrison plot was Mrs. Carol Aydelotte, who, as mentioned earlier, supplied Garrison with the photograph of Gene Bradley that was identified by former Dallas County Deputy Sheriff Roger Craig.

Mrs. Aydelotte was perhaps the most fanatical of the lot. She was known as the "den mother" of the Minutemen, and for a time Dennis Mower lived at her home. Her circle of close associates included Philip Earl Scheib and Loran Eugene Hall, whom she knew as Lorenzo Pascillo. Her range of activities in fanatical right-wing movements included involvement with the American Nazi Party and the John Birch Society. Her husband, Art, was once arrested by police for concealing an arsenal of weapons and ammunition in their home.

Carol Aydelotte didn't just pick Gene Bradley's name and picture out of the blue. As Bradley told the story, Mrs. Aydelotte heard his name mentioned in right-wing circles and came to him seeking a handout for one of her more unusual causes. According to Bradley, he called Mrs. Aydelotte and her supporters "kooks" and from that day forward the woman spurned became his mortal enemy.

Bradley said he was astonished to learn that Mrs. Aydelotte labeled him a Communist at a meeting of the local John Birch Society in North Hollywood and also accused him of committing a number of violent crimes, including murder.

Bradley told me that his neighbors started picking up the whispered rumors, and when he could stand it no longer—after all, he worked for a far-right movement—he wrote a letter to Robert Welch, national leader of the Birchers, demanding that the little old candy-maker from Massachusetts conduct an investigation of his bittersweet North Hollywood chapter. According to Bradley, Welch flew to Los Angeles promptly, investigated the North Hollywood chapter, and then made a number of changes in the leadership, which included downgrading Carol Aydelotte.

From that moment forward Bradley's life became a living hell. Mrs. Aydelotte sued him for slander, charging that Bradley had depicted her as a procurer of men and that he had accused her of plotting to murder her mother for money.

In his countersuit Bradley charged that Mrs. Aydelotte had deliberately smeared him by accusing him of rape and murder. He quoted her as once saying that he had had a part in the murder of the Reverend Dallas Roquemore in Weaverville, California.

Gene Bradley spoke the truth. Mrs. Aydelotte and her followers in the Minutemen tried at various times to implicate him in three other murders apart from the assassination of John Kennedy.

Why was such an effort made to finger Gene Bradley as the mystery man in Dealey Plaza? Why was Gene Brading excluded from this macabre picture?

From a personal standpoint I was saddened—perhaps troubled is a better word—by the fact that such breast-beating organizations as the American Civil Liberties Union would not lift a finger to help Gene Bradley, nor would the straight-laced libertarians in the United States Justice Department, who were well aware of Jim Garrison's evil machinations.

Gene Bradley was an auxiliary policeman in the city of Burbank, but none of his fellow officers came forward in his defense. Among his closest friends were a number of FBI agents from the Los Angeles bureau. They wouldn't even discuss the case.

Perhaps if Gene Bradley were a bleeding-heart liberal, the ACLU and the Justice Department would have beaten their legal drums on his behalf. But he had no such luck.

It strikes me as a matter of cataclysmic proportions that the only entry made in Bradley's defense in the public record is contained on a card filed in the LAPD's intelligence unit, which says, "Edgar Eugene Bradley, North Hollywood, Calif. The man Garrison mistook for Eugene Hale Brading AKA Jim Braden."

XVII

AFTER THE FACT

In the fall of 1963 the man known as Jim Braden was not exactly a symbol of affluence. He had been thrown out of his former wife's Palm Springs mansion and was living in an apartment in West Los Angeles—a real comedown. But in the winter of 1964 there seemed to be a complete turn-around in his financial condition. Almost overnight he was leading a life of leisure on the country-club circuit, squiring wealthy widows and divorcées and acquiring property.

But there was one incident that detracted from the good life. On February 10, 1964, Braden was arrested for shoplifting at a market in the San Fernando Valley. It was pretty much of an embarrassment for a high roller with access to organized crime's ruling hierarchy as well as to some rather substantial names in big business. Bing Crosby and Bob Hope might well have been shocked to learn that a fellow member in one of Southern California's most exclusive clubs had been picked up on such a petty charge. The arrest report routinely noted that Braden was taken into custody at a Safeway store, 21909 Ventura Boulevard, Woodland Hills, California, under Section 484 of the State Penal Code. A store detective told police he had seen Mr. Braden wheel a shopping cart containing about twenty to twenty-five dollars worth of groceries out the main entrance of the market. According to police records, Braden insisted that shoplifting was the furthest thing from his mind.

He said he had a bad cold and was so congested that he was forced to go outside the store so he could spit in the street. Braden was carrying a substantial amount of money in his wallet, the arresting officer noted, and frantically offered to make a cash settlement on the spot. But the store detective was adamant and insisted that the police jail Braden on suspicion of shoplifting.

Braden told the arresting officer he lived at 621 South Barrington Avenue, West Los Angeles—a distance of about fifteen miles from the market where he was arrested. It seemed like a long way to go for shopping. He was fingerprinted, photographed, and then released on bail. The next day Braden appeared in court and informed the presiding judge that he wanted to plead guilty because he didn't want to be bothered with a lawyer. He was given a suspended sixty-day jail sentence, fined fifty dollars, and placed on two years' probation. (At the time of the incident he was still on federal probation for having swindled Mrs. Gertrude Joyce).

Since fingerprints were taken, the pertinent details of the arrest were sent routinely to FBI headquarters in Washington, where a computer brought out the fact that Eugene Hale Brading and Jim Braden were one and the same person. That, of course, was the first time Brading's FBI rap sheet, No. 799 431, showed the alias of Jim Braden. But apparently the only place where that information was known was in the computer's memory bank.

Only thirteen days prior to the shoplifting incident, FBI agents Chester C. Orton and John K. Anderson interviewed Braden in Los Angeles about the events in Dealey Plaza, without the slightest inkling that he was the notorious Eugene Hale Brading. Apparently the name of Braden was not submitted to FBI headquarters in Washington for a perfunctory check. If it had been, Orton and Anderson would eventually have learned that Braden and Brading were one and the same man. When I attempted to learn more about the interview with Braden from the FBI office in Los Angeles, I was told that agent Orton was dead but that I was free to talk to Anderson if he consented. Anderson told me he could not recall the interview, that Chester Orton had been in charge of the investigation. So if there were any more details beyond the official FBI report, Orton took them to the grave.

Why did Eugene Brading make the slip in the Safeway market? If he hadn't, he most likely would not have been revealed (with complete certainty) as the Jim Braden taken into custody in Dealey Plaza. One school of thought holds that Brading was "rousted" in the market; that Los Angeles police intelligence officers—well ac-acquainted with his hoodlum past—set him up on the shoplifting charge. It was pretty much common knowledge that when such Mafia types as Jimmy Fratianno set foot in Los Angeles, police put a tail on them. A second school of thought—one subscribed to by homicide detectives investigating Robert Kennedy's murder—holds that Brading was simply a petty thief at heart, despite his bountiful interests, and that he couldn't resist the opportunity to swipe a cart of groceries.

Brading's parole officer bought the second theory, contending that no matter how much affluence and status a congenital thief achieves, he never changes his stripes. Federal officials did not deem the shoplifting offense serious enough to revoke Brading's parole.

I subscribe to a third theory—that Brading was telling the truth for once, that he had the severe cold he described and needed to clear his throat. A bad cough and a stuffed-up nose may be the simple explanation for a twist of fate that gave Eugene Hale Brading a new identity on his FBI arrest record. However, if he was indeed just trying to clear his throat, why didn't he leave the cart inside?

Brading was far from being a pauper after John Kennedy was assassinated. In January of 1964 he became a charter member of the elegant La Costa Country Club, about thirty miles south of Richard Nixon's Western White House, at San Clemente. As far as law-enforcement officers throughout California were concerned, La Costa was a citadel of organized crime. Once again using the name *Jim Braden,* Brading took out membership card NB 135 at La Costa. His ex-wife, Mildred Bollman, who had already regretted the haste with which she had evicted Brading from her Palm Springs mansion, likewise became a charter member of the hoodlum spa by the sea.

The fact that Brading was accepted into La Costa indicated that he was a person of stature, since the membership was almost entirely made up of celebrities from either the entertainment industry or organized crime.

In the period before and after the JFK assassination, Brading seemed to become involved in a multitude of financial interests. There was the substantial increase for the month of November 1963 in the revenue from his oil well in Louisiana. Apart from his office at 215 South La Cienega Boulevard, Beverly Hills, Brading had still another interest in an oil investment firm at 8249 Beverly Boulevard, Beverly Hills, where old friend Roger Bauman—who had tweaked the curiosity of Los Angeles police intelligence officers many years before—did business under the name of Bauman and Burke.

Together, Bauman and Brading directed the activities of the Bauman Drilling Company, in Louisiana, with holdings that supposedly included a number of gas and oil leases in Acadia

Parish. The headquarters for the Bauman-Brading operation was the Gulf State Building, in Dallas. (One might recall at this point that Brading told FBI agents Chester Orton and John Anderson that he was not familiar with Dallas.)

In 1964 Brading and Bauman expanded their financial holdings to include the B&B Cattle Company in Chicago, a firm ostensibly set up in Monmouth, Illinois, to deal in the commodity market. Although *B&B* reportedly stood for Bauman and Brading, neither man was listed as an officer in the corporation. Brading was said to have advised federal parole authorities that he put up $25,000 as his share of capital in the company but that it was a bad gamble and he lost most of the money.

Sometime in the same period Brading invested $39,000 in two lots at the exclusive Coral Gables Estates Club, in Coral Gables, Florida. Parole officials were under the impression that ex-wife Mildred Bollman was hoping for a marital reconciliation and had started to keep company with Brading once more, despite her experience in Palm Springs. Brading was desperately trying to have his parole terminated during this period of new-found affluence. He had even written a letter to parole authorities stating that he and a doctor were vying for the affections of a well-to-do widow from St. Louis and asking that his parole be lifted so that he would be in a much better position to compete with the man of medicine.

Brading told friends that he and Millie

planned to build a honeymoon home in Coral Gables and retire there to a life of leisure. He even showed parole officials a picture of a home in *House Beautiful* magazine and said that he intended to build one like it in Coral Gables. Brading's initial efforts to purchase the land at Coral Gables were rebuffed by operators of the development, who somehow found out about his hoodlum background and said they did not want him polluting the landscape. Nevertheless, Brading brought pressure—and influence—to bear on club officials, and they knuckled under and sold him the property after he paid them $39,000 in cash. After all, he was an oil man from Beverly Hills, California.

If there was any romance with Millie Bollman, it was short-lived, for there is no record that they ever took up bed and board together in Coral Gables. With his new-found status on the country-club circuit, Brading found a stable of divorcées and rich widows.

His parole was terminated in 1965, and he was free to come and go as he pleased. He acquired a new home for himself at a development near the La Costa Country Club. He also purchased an inexpensive home for his parents in Santa Barbara.

He took up golf and had one of the lowest handicaps on the links at La Costa. He was known as a swinger on and off the course.

He traveled frequently and still maintained the façade of a legitimate businessman. He acquired a new office at 280 South Beverly Drive, Beverly Hills, but was seldom seen there. He described himself as a representative of the Empire Oil and Regency Company of Louisiana, and when interrogated by state agents, he insisted that he was not connected with any California concerns.

His associates in Room 402 of the somber gray office building in Beverly Hills included a cadre of connivers. Three other men in Brading's office were implicated in a 1968 plot to bribe Los Angeles City Councilman Thomas Shepherd to obtain a zoning change on a fairly substantial parcel of land in the San Fernando Valley. The money was minimal by mob standards—only $10,000. Shepherd ultimately was convicted, but Brading's office associates, J. M. Arnoff, Wallace White, and Gerald Chace, went free because they turned state's evidence and chirped like canaries to the Los Angeles County Grand Jury.

An investigator once asked me if I thought Brading might have been involved in the bribery activities spawned in Room 402. My answer was that a man who had attained his stature couldn't be bothered. On the few occasions that Brading did show up at the office he looked as if he had just gotten off the tennis courts and was headed for a big evening on the town.

Intelligence officers were frequently attracted to Brading's activities because of his links to illegal gambling and because of his ability to mesmerize rich widows. One such widow, a sophisticated lady from Dallas whose name need not be mentioned in this investigation, fell into Brading's clutches, and in no time at all, they were married in a lavish formal ceremony. Just as quickly the marriage was dissolved. In early 1969 the widow told investigators that Brading had taken her for about $50,000 but that she would have considered it cheap at twice the price. The widow, whose first husband had owned a lucrative automobile agency in Dallas, noted that Brading was a man of no definite political persuasion but a social animal who moved continuously on the country-club circuit.

To police he was a man of mystery who had acquired huge sums of money without visible means of support, apart from what he obtained on occasion from a wealthy widow. Investigators acknowledged that he had been in Dallas when John Kennedy was assassinated and in Los Angeles when Robert Kennedy was slain. The latter appearance could be explained away—at least to the satisfaction of Los Angeles police. But the appearance in Dallas was a mind-boggler.

Furthermore, intelligence officers considered Brading to have much more significance than did their counterparts in homicide, who were investigating the RFK assassination. To intelligence he was one of the ranking figures in the underworld; to homicide he was a petty con man once picked up for shoplifting.

The fact that Eugene Hale Brading had surfaced at the La Costa Country Club after the JFK assassination was doubly significant to intelligence. His money, his bankroll, and his investments circa 1964 may or may not have come from the purses of wealthy widows. But the fact that he was a charter member of La Costa seemed to demonstrate conclusively that his star was shining brightly in the world of organized crime.

XVIII

IN RETROSPECT

This had indeed been a curious investigation. Every time I leafed through a page in Eugene Hale Brading's life story I was intrigued with what I found—one unanswered question after another, coincidence after coincidence—a web so intricately woven it seemed impossible to disentangle.

Some of my associates at CBS openly discouraged me from exploring the situation. Initially, most of them were intrigued with the Garrison investigation in New Orleans, and two of my colleagues, David Browning and Paul Udell, spent considerable time in Louisiana trying to understand—or unravel—the story that had been offered the American people as a solution to John Kennedy's murder. But the facts didn't add up, and like most other newsmen, Browning and Udell quickly soured on Jim Garrison. Their attitudes were symptomatic of the waning interest in the JFK assassination—a by-product, for the most part, of the incredible Garrison investigation.

What I have written is not an indictment of anyone. Indictments can only be returned by Grand Juries. The only Grand Jury to consider the JFK assassination was the one convened by Jim Garrison in New Orleans. And in the light of what is now known, it appears conceivable that Garrison had stacked the deck right from the start.

Consider these facts. At this writing Jim Garrison is awaiting trial for bribery, corruption, and tax-evasion. The government insists he has been taking payoffs from organized crime in New Orleans for years.

Yet here is a man who pompously proclaimed that he had solved the mystery of the assassination of President John Fitzgerald Kennedy, and in so doing, virtually destroyed the lives of innocent men by branding them with the stigma of an assassination conspiracy.

As for Eugene Hale Brading, his life is every bit as tumultuous as that of the New Orleans District Attorney. Brading is under investigation by numerous agencies, including a Federal Strike Force from Washington, D. C., investigating organized crime in both Las Vegas and Southern California, the Internal Revenue Service, the state of California, and the state of Nevada. (The Nevada Gaming Board, which monitors the activities of all casinos in the state, is specifically interested in Brading.)

The principal focus of all these agencies is on

Brading's role as a suspected courier for organized crime.

Perhaps Brading is nothing more than a petty con man whose fleecing skills were used to advantage by the real masterminds of organized crime. Certainly law-enforcement officers with expertise in this area give Brading mixed reviews. Some consider him capable of anything. Others note that he has never been connected, at least publicly, with violent crime, although they concede this is not the case with many of his associates.

There are some who firmly believe that Brading may not have actually known why he was in Dealey Plaza on November 22, 1963, and at this point, one must concede that possibility.

I am convinced that everything I have written is a completely honest and documented bill of particulars—one that asks the question: did the Mafia kill Kennedy? And further: did the men who pull the strings in organized crime carry out the crime of the century in collusion with fanatical, right-wing extremists?

I have presented evidence that was never explored by the Warren Commission, at least according to the records it made public. Individual members of the FBI and various intelligence agencies have acknowledged that this is for the most part new information. Yet they have been reluctant to reopen the JFK investigation or even consider the merits of this new information. I am convinced that certain key people in the United

States Department of Justice do not want to concede the possibility of error in the JFK investigation.

As I write this final chapter, it has been nearly ten years since John Kennedy's life was snuffed out in Dealey Plaza. I remember only too well the chill that ran through my body when the first news bulletin of the assassination flashed over my car radio as I drove to work that day. One of the first things I thought of was my meeting with John Kennedy in Los Angeles in 1959, when he was still a Senator. The meeting took place at the Biltmore Hotel, following a dreadfully dull Democratic fund-raising dinner, at which John Kennedy was supposed to be the featured speaker, though he was upstaged by every hack politician in Southern California.

Jack Kennedy was a warm, inviting person. He avoided cheap political talk. He was interested in people and places, and he talked about both. It appeared that he felt at home in the company of reporters. In the background Jacqueline Kennedy stared coldly at the assembled newsmen. Her stare appeared to grow more chilly every time her husband reached for a drink. But Jack Kennedy paid no heed to her obvious annoyance. One reporter suddenly became quite serious during the light-hearted conversation and said, "Senator, you might make a good President." His only response was, "You really think so?"

And on November 22, 1963—four years later—

this man of promise was dead, and like millions of other Americans, I cried.

The information in this book was unraveled slowly down a tortuous, convoluted path. The Warren Commission had zeroed in on H. L. Hunt and his sons during the investigation. At first I was reluctant to believe that Brading and three of his colleagues had visited the Hunt Oil Company offices in Dallas the day before the assassination and that Jack Ruby had also been there that same day. But then the facts came to light. There was documentation in federal parole files that the announced purpose of Brading's visit to Dallas was to see Lamar Hunt on oil business. Why then, when questioned years later, did he deny going to the offices of Lamar and Nelson Hunt?

It is not equally puzzling that Jack Ruby put in an appearance at the offices of the Hunt Oil Company on the same day?

There can be no doubting that Eugene Hale Brading was a member of the organized underworld. The documentation is beyond dispute. It is a fact that he was present in Dealey Plaza on November 22, 1963, acting suspiciously enough to be taken to the Dallas County Sheriff's station for questioning. Not once did he volunteer his true identity, not in Dallas after the assassination, nor in Los Angeles when questioned by FBI agents the following January. What, if anything, did Eugene Hale Brading have to hide? Why did he change the identification on his California driver's license two months before he appeared in Dallas? Why did he first try to identify himself with a credit card instead of his driver's license?

Jim Garrison's investigation of Edgar Eugene Bradley appears questionable, to say the least. The very fact that Garrison attempted to bring Bradley to trial for the murder of John Kennedy was significant. Garrison has bitterly denounced newsmen for constantly carping about his alleged ties to the Mafia and overlooking the "evidence" he produced in his investigation. Why then didn't Garrison identify David Ferrie for what he was— a working member of Carlos Marcello's Mafia empire in New Orleans?

What could have possibly motivated Garrison to ignore Eugene Hale Brading during the investigation in New Orleans?

Why did members of the fanatical paramilitary group known as the Minutemen come forward to assist Garrison in his conspiracy investigation by fingering Edgar Eugene Bradley? One member of that group—a man who volunteered his services to Garrison—was positively identified by two Warren Commission witnesses as traveling with Lee Harvey Oswald in both Dallas and New Orleans prior to the assassination. That man, of course, was Loran Eugene Hall.

By its own admission, Loran Eugene Hall was unfinished business as far as the Warren Commission was concerned. The testimony linking him to Oswald was never satisfactorily refuted. Would the average county prosecutor dealing with a murder case ignore such pointed evidence? But to the Warren Commission, both Eugene Hale Brading and Loran Eugene Hall were obscure footnotes to history, or, better yet, trivia to be ignored.

Was Oswald a member of the Minutemen? There is room for debate on this question. Scratch your memory bank and recall that photograph of Oswald posing with a mail-order rifle. That is a typical Minuteman pose. Some have suggested that the photograph was a fraud and have submitted detailed evidence to support their contention. I have not attempted to examine this subject. It does not seem that important. But I wonder what could have motivated anyone to doctor such a photograph.

Is there a possibility that Brading can be linked directly to the Minutemen? Not at this moment, although his closest associate Victor Emanuel Pereira, was well acquainted with Philip Earl Scheib, one of the leaders of the Minuteman movement in Southern California. Pereira, of course, was the business partner of the young paramilitarist's father, Earl Scheib, the cut-rate carpainter. And Philip Earl Scheib was no stranger to assassination plots, having actually been arrested by the FBI during the course of one such investigation.

Is there a possibility that Brading knew David Ferrie? While eyewitnesses are lacking—at least no one has been willing to come forward—such would appear to be the case. Brading and Ferrie worked a few feet away from each other in the

Père Marquette Building in New Orleans in the fall of 1963. Both were associated with the higher echelons of organized crime in the United States. And both were noted for the "brain power" they supplied to the Mafia.

Was David Ferrie acquainted with Lee Harvey Oswald? The evidence strongly suggests that he was. Why did Oswald use that Camp Street address on his Fair Play for Cuba literature? That address was the headquarters of the noted right-winger Guy Bannister and his associate, Jack Martin—the latter being the person who implicated Ferrie in John Kennedy's murder. Ferrie was no stranger to the Camp Street office. Oswald, in all probability, did not pull that address out of a hat.

With all this in mind it strikes me as slightly unusual that most investigators—including Earl Warren—ignored the significance of Jack Ruby's execution of Lee Harvey Oswald while the President's assassin was being removed from the Dallas City Jail. Ruby had long been associated with members of the organized underworld. That, too, is a matter of public record. How can anyone accept his lame excuse that he executed Oswald so that Jacqueline Kennedy would not have to return to Dallas for the murder trial? Jack Ruby was a man who wallowed in the gutter of vice and corruption. His movements in Dallas on the day of the assassination are questionable, to say the least. Evidence in the Warren Commission's own findings strongly suggests that Ruby was present at Parkland Hospital when the mortally wounded President was wheeled into the operating room. This Ruby denied. Why?

Furthermore, there is the proximity of Oswald's Dallas rooming house to Ruby's apartment. There is a strong possibility that when Ruby pumped the fatal bullet into Oswald's body, they were not strangers in the night.

Why and how did NBC news obtain information about David Ferrie so early in the investigation of the assassination? Why would Ferrie try to blame Oswald's actions in Dealey Plaza on a hypnotist at Jack Ruby's Carousel Club? All this is more than just curious coincidence.

Two groups are closely interwoven in this investigation: the organized underworld and para-military extremists. Both groups hated the Kennedy family. The organized underworld, led by Carlos Marcello and Meyer Lansky, had good reason—Marcello because he had been unceremoniously kicked out of the United States by Robert Kennedy, Lansky because his financial peccadillos were generating increasing interest in the United States Justice Department through the prodding of the Kennedys, thereby threatening his iron grip on Las Vegas and on the millions he was pocketing.

The hatred on the part of the Minutemen was the typical paranoia associated with fanatics, whether of the far right or the extreme left. Someone once remarked to me that Thomas Paine was the first of the virulent extremists who set the pattern for the many fanatical groups in our history, such as the Minutemen.

As I have said before, it is a convoluted path. Now, ten years after the assassination of John Kennedy, I cannot for one moment accept the proposition that he was killed by Lee Harvey Oswald acting as a solitary killer. Perhaps I cannot refute the findings of the Warren Commission with perfect certainty at this point. But I challenge any member of that Commission to refute what I have written and explain the obvious mistakes in the original investigation.

Explain to me why the investigation of "Jim Braden" was so inadequate. Explain why the initial reports about David Ferrie were dismissed out of hand. Explain why the investigation of Loran Eugene Hall was not completed by the time the Warren Commission went to press. Explain why Earl Warren turned down Jack Ruby's request for safe conduct out of Dallas so he could tell the truth about the Kennedy assassination.

There have been more myths associated with the events in Dealey Plaza than with perhaps any other crime in history. Many of those myths were the product of the fertile but devious mind of Jim Garrison. The New Orleans D.A. was the principal architect of the story that the CIA plotted the assassination of John Kennedy. It is true that the story was first nurtured by others, but credit for its fermentation belongs to Garrison.

Another myth is that President Lyndon Johnson masterminded the assassination—an ugly lie that must be rejected completely. Johnson himself feared that he might be accused of involvement in such a conspiracy.

It is easy to pull any number of theories out of a hat. One can speculate endlessly about that dark moment in Dallas. It is another thing to present evidence which might conceivably alter the Warren Commission's finding that, lacking anything more conclusive in the way of information, it must be presumed that Lee Harvey Oswald acted alone in carrying out the assassination of President John Fitzgerald Kennedy.

I suggest that it is not too late to revive this ugly moment in America's history. A Congressional committee, armed with the power of subpoena, could give the American people an opportunity to live with the truth again. Earl Warren had no right to tell the American people that they might not know the truth about the assassination in their lifetime.

All I ask is that the facts be examined from start to finish. Was Eugene Hale Brading's rise to prominence in the organized underworld connected with his presence in Dealey Plaza on November 22, 1963? Or was his being there just an accident of history? One way or the other, the American people are entitled to an answer.

XIX

POSTSCRIPT RFK

Before he too was killed by an assassin's bullets on June 6, 1968, it was generally thought that Senator Robert Kennedy was satisfied with the results of the Warren Commission's investigation into his brother's death in Dealey Plaza. At least that was the impression he conveyed publicly.

But actually, that impression was far removed from reality. Robert Kennedy had lingering doubts about the solitary-assassin theory advocated by the Warren Commission. For many months after that day in Dallas, Robert Kennedy was numb with grief. And initially that numbness led to his quiet acceptance of the Warren Commission's investigation.

But in the spring of 1967 that numbness seemed to vanish overnight. As a United States Senator from New York, he picked up the mantle of the Kennedy legacy and began a feverish bid for the Presidency of the United States. It was then that he began to convey his private doubts about the Warren Commission. While expressing pessimism about the Commission's findings, the Senator refused to deal with specifics in discussing the assassination, even with his most trusted aides.

There was one person, however, who became extremely close to Robert Kennedy, and became privy to the Senator's lingering doubts. This man, who asked that his name not be revealed, eventually determined that Robert Kennedy was conducting his own personal investigation of his brother's assassination.

The Senator explained that something had occurred in Southern California that had bothered him a great deal; something that should have been investigated by the Warren Commission, but wasn't. When pressed for specifics, the Senator replied that he was particularly bothered by the contents of an Associated Press story from Oxnard, California, on November 23, 1963—the day after his brother's assassination.

Here is that story:

Oxnard, California (AP)—A telephone company executive said that 20 minutes before President Kennedy was assassinated a woman caller was overheard whispering:

"The President is going to be killed."

Ray Sheehan, manager of the Oxnard division of General Telephone Company, said the caller "stumbled into our operator's circuits," perhaps by misdialing.

Sheehan said the woman "seemed to be a little bit disturbed." Besides predicting the

President's death, he said, she "mumbled several incoherent things."

Sheehan said the call was reported to the Federal Bureau of Investigation in Los Angeles but not until after the President had been shot. Until then, he said, it appeared to have been just another crank call.

Sheehan said there was no way to trace the call. All he could say was that it originated in the Oxnard-Camarillo area some 50 miles north of Los Angeles.

The FBI in Los Angeles declined to comment.

Sheehan said one telephone supervisor called another one onto her line after getting the call. He said both supervisors heard the woman say the President would be killed.

Sheehan said the call was received at 10:10 A.M., Pacific Time. The President was shot in Dallas shortly after 10:30 A.M.

Sheehan said he doesn't think the caller was ever connected with another party. He said she may not have known she had supervisors on the line and may have just been talking to no one in particular.

Robert Kennedy felt that unless the woman caller heard by the telephone supervisors was clairvoyant, there was sufficient reason to suspect she might have knowledge of an assassination plot. It bothered him no end.

In May of 1968 Robert Kennedy was campaigning up and down the West Coast in a hectic scramble for votes in the Democratic Presidential primaries in California and Oregon, which pitted him against Senator Eugene McCarthy of Minnesota. During a campaign stop in Oregon, Kennedy confided to a friend that when he reached the Los Angeles area he intended to stop off in Oxnard and see if he could learn anything more about that mysterious telephone call.

On May 28, 1968, the Senator and his party flew into Oxnard. His advisers and campaign aides hardly gave it a second thought when he disappeared for two hours. He was tense; it had been rough going in Oregon, where the voters had been more receptive to Gene McCarthy.

When Kennedy returned, an aide inquired where he had gone. The Senator laughed and said he had lost his hat while campaigning and had spent the two hours trying to find it. That was the end of the conversation. But can anyone remember Robert Kennedy covering his touseled hair with a headpiece as he campaigned for votes? What Kennedy was doing in Oxnard was attempting to find out more about that phone call.

His prolonged visit to Oxnard that day delayed his return to Oregon and the final campaign showdown with Gene McCarthy. The press statements said Kennedy's plane was delayed by heavy fog. But the real reason for the delay was Bobby Kennedy's gut feeling that somewhere in Southern California lay the answer to his brother's murder in Dallas.

What, if anything, Bobby learned in Oxnard was never determined. A few days later in Los Angeles, shortly after midnight on June 5, 1968, history repeated itself. A mousy little gunman leaped out of the shadows at the Ambassador Hotel and mortally wounded Robert Kennedy, moments after he had claimed victory in the California primary.

His name was Sirhan Bishara Sirhan, and like Lee Harvey Oswald he was immediately depicted as a dedicated Marxist. Like Oswald, Sirhan had kept a diary in which he professed his allegiance to Communism. In it he wrote, "RFK must die" over and over again. It was paradoxical that Sirhan was suddenly a Marxist. Four years before, while attending Pasadena City College, he had openly advocated the election of conservative Senator Barry Goldwater as President. Although born in Jordan, Sirhan was considered Americanized by every standard.

He wanted to drive fast cars, wear expensive clothes, and date beautiful women. He was only five feet three inches tall and weighed 120 pounds; but he envisioned himself as bigger than king size.

Sirhan had an obsession with money, which was noted in his diary when he wrote: "Please pay to the order of Sirhan. . . . Please pay to the order of Sirhan."

He was a man of many faces and posed intriguing possibilities for the writer who was to become Sirhan's personal biographer, Robert Blair Kaiser.

Under an arrangement worked out with Sirhan's lawyers, Kaiser became an investigator for the defense—a move that enabled him to have access to all records dealing with the case. Kaiser agreed to a three-way split of the proceeds from the book. One-third would go to the Sirhan family, another third to the defense lawyers, and the rest to Kaiser.

Kaiser's finished product, *RFK Must Die* (Random House), ran 634 pages; yet it failed to shed any light on the assassin's motives. Kaiser convinced himself that Sirhan was involved in a conspiracy, but he was at a loss to explain precisely who the conspirators might be. He noted that Sirhan was attracted to the Black Panthers, whose leaders espoused assassination. Kaiser also maintained that Sirhan had connections with both organized crime and right-wing extremists.

But in the long run, Sirhan was more difficult to track than Lee Harvey Oswald, and Kaiser knew it.

Sirhan had indeed toyed with the black militant movement, and according to one informant, he had attended a meeting of the Black Panthers in South-Central Los Angeles two weeks before Robert Kennedy was murdered. But according to the informant, the Panthers ejected Sirhan from the meeting.

Sirhan's best friend, Walter Crowe, was a dedicated Communist. But according to Crowe, he could never interest Sirhan in the radical brand of Marxism he preached.

As for the radical right, plenty of names were thrown around in the police investigation, but conclusive evidence of a conspiracy was always lacking. The name of Minuteman Keith Gilbert, whose closest associates were deeply involved in the Garrison investigation in New Orleans, was among the more prominent, even though he was in San Quentin Prison at the time of the RFK assassination.

One of those handcuffed by police shortly after Robert Kennedy was shot was a young student from Los Angeles City College, Michael Wayne, who vaguely resembled Sirhan Sirhan. In checking out the name of Michael Wayne at police headquarters, investigators found it cross-indexed to Keith Gilbert. At the time Gilbert had been implicated in the plot to kill Dr. Martin Luther King, police had found the calling card of a Michael Wayne in the garage of the Minuteman's Glendale residence. After several hundred manhours of investigation, the police finally satisfied themselves that the Michael Wayne connected with Keith Gilbert was someone entirely different from the youth taken into custody at the Ambassador Hotel.

As for organized crime, there was only one theory that intrigued the LAPD, and that was the possibility that Eugene Hale Brading might in some way be connected with Sirhan Bishara Sirhan. Chief of Detectives, Robert Houghton, called it the "most complex conspiratorial material" to confront his detectives. Houghton had reason to wonder whether Sirhan might be wedded to the organized underworld. The first attorney to step forward to defend Sirhan was Russell Parsons, a brilliant criminal attorney who had frequently defended members of that underworld and was a bitter enemy of Robert Kennedy. Among his more notorious Mafia clients was Joseph Sica. Parsons had once run for Mayor of Los Angeles, but his political career was short-lived; it was discovered he had written a letter to authorities in Cleveland, Ohio, stating that Mickey Cohen had "rehabilitated" himself and recommending that his probation on criminal charges be terminated. At that time Cohen was fighting with Jimmy Fratianno for control of the organized underworld in Los Angeles.

Parsons' hatred of Robert Kennedy dated back to the time Bobby served as counsel for the Senate Rackets Committee. Kennedy was particularly interested in Parsons' hoodlum connections, and he even went so far as to check out the lawyer's bank records.

Immediately after Parsons was named counsel for Sirhan, he created a nationwide furor when he said that the little assassin was getting praise from a number of people who thought he had "done a good thing."

Parsons' chief investigator on the Sirhan case was a one-time crooked cop, Michael McCowan, who had been convicted of mail theft while serving on the department, and had also been involved in a massive real estate fraud in the San Fernando Valley.

Bob Houghton worried about these facts, and when he discovered the story about Eugene Hale Brading in Dealey Plaza his concern mounted. Houghton's investigators pored over every facet of Brading's life. They could not find one link to Sirhan, but in the course of their detailed probe several of them became convinced that Brading had some explaining to do about his presence in Dealey Plaza on November 22, 1963.

A number of lawyers and private investigators, as of this writing, have filed court suits to force the LAPD to make a full disclosure of its records in the Sirhan case. The records consist of ten volumes covering every phase of the investigation. I am convinced that the department will never make the records public voluntarily because it fears the information in its possession concerning Eugene Hale Brading is potentially explosive. Even should a court order the LAPD to release the ten volumes, I am willing to wager that the hundreds of pages dealing with the mystery man of Dealey Plaza will somehow disappear. For one thing, certain officials in the United States Justice Department do not want the information made public so long after the fact.

I disagree. It is never too late to know the truth or at least to try to find it. Maybe Earl Warren will be proved wrong in our lifetime.

XX

WHERE THE ACTION IS

The very fact that Eugene Hale Brading, using the alias of Jim Braden, was a charter member of the La Costa Country Club (initial membership fee $2,500) made him one of the more celebrated figures in the organized underworld. Once a petty thief and swindler of portly but wealthy widows, his ascension to prominence at La Costa placed him in a league with the legendary Meyer Lansky.

Nestled in the rolling green countryside two miles from the blue Pacific, the Rancho La Costa development is a monument to the Mafia—the organized underworld.

The 3,000-acre spa by the sea, financed by one of James Hoffa's Teamsters Union pension funds, is where the action is in California. On occasion, intelligence officers have bumped into each other while snooping on the premises. Chances are that a doorman is either a police informant or a distant relative of Lucky Luciano. Like Las Vegas, La Costa is "open territory"—meaning no specific

Mafia family retains control over it. But the brains behind La Costa are clearly visible.

It was often said that the arrival of industrialist Howard Hughes in Las Vegas was like a breath of fresh desert air, since the bashful billionaire bought up almost every casino in sight, thereby enabling the mob to make a graceful exit from the gambling mecca. Hughes acquired one mob-owned casino after another, and Nevada politicians openly boasted that the Mafia had departed the scene. (Later those same politicians bemoaned the fact that Hughes had tried to bring a "family" atmosphere to Las Vegas—sort of a Disneyland in the desert—and had thereby caused a loss in gambling revenue. There just wasn't enough action on the Strip to suit the highrollers. The politicians and businessmen conceded privately that what Las Vegas needed was a little bit of the old-fashioned vice and corruption that made it a landmark in years gone by.)

The real powerhouses in the Vegas underworld didn't travel far. Like the hearty pioneers a century before, they simply trekked across the border to California, where they settled down at Rancho La Costa in baronial style. Once this modern-day Xanadu began taking shape with the help of Teamsters funds, it became the favorite gathering spot for mobsters from all over the nation, as well as for many politicians, judges, and prominent members of the entertainment industry.

The driving force behind La Costa was Morris B. "Moe" Dalitz. Dalitz operated the Desert Inn in Las Vegas, before selling it to Hughes, who subsequently sequestered himself in the penthouse with shades drawn day and night.

Mention Moe Dalitz and you mention a name in organized crime that is equated with the likes of Al Capone, Lucky Luciano, and Meyer Lansky. Dalitz has more in common with Lansky than with the others, since both are considered experts in financial affairs. Although both men are Jewish, the Italian branch of the Mafia family considers both Lansky and Dalitz to be the "royalty" of the organized underworld and treats them with great respect.

Had Eugene Hale Brading been a bush-league petty thief, he would not have wound up in the select group of 100 persons chosen to be charter members in Moe Dalitz' La Costa Country Club.

Before 1947, when he acquired a 74 percent interest in the Desert Inn in Las Vegas (at a cost of $1,300,000), Dalitz based his operations in Cleveland, where he was known as the leader of the Mayfield Road Gang. According to an intelligence report, anyone who questioned Dalitz' power in Cleveland "would have to deal with Lucky Luciano, Bugsy Siegal, and Meyer Lansky."

The same intelligence report said that Dalitz' move to Las Vegas was the direct result of pressure brought to bear on him by one of the most famous crime-fighters in the United States, Eliott Ness, who was appointed Public Safety Director of Cleveland when the Mayfield Road Gang was in its heyday.

Dalitz' most trusted lieutenant in Las Vegas was Allard Roen, who ran the Stardust Hotel until he pleaded guilty in Federal Court to stock swindling, which made him a convicted felon and ineligible under Nevada law to hold a casino license.

Like Eugene Hale Brading, Allard Roen was a charter member of La Costa. So were Jack Donnelley, an attorney who oversaw Moe Dalitz' legal problems in Las Vegas; John Allessio, the San Diego gambling kingpin and industrial tycoon, who in 1971 was sentenced to federal prison after he pleaded guilty to skimming off millions from his racetrack interests; John "Jake the Barber" Factor, a relic of Al Capone's days in Chicago, who acquired a fortune in West Coast real estate and became known as a gentleman philanthropist; Jimmy Blankenship; Mervyn Adelson; Nathan Adelson; and others of similar persuasion.

On the celebrity side of the ledger, big names abounded. Topping the list were Bob Hope, Bing Crosby, Frank Sinatra, Desi Arnaz, and Hoagy Carmichael.

It was a happy blend of the best of two worlds —organized crime and the entertainment industry.

The fact that Moe Dalitz was at the helm of La Costa triggered massive surveillance by local law-enforcement officers as well as the FBI and the United States Justice Department. Intelligence files showed that a number of prominent political figures and judges were "freeloading" guests at La Costa, with Moe Dalitz picking up the tab for their accommodations. Among them were a prominent United States Senator from the East Coast, known in politics as an ardent liberal, a Federal Court appeals judge from Washington, D. C., and a member of the State Supreme Court of Nevada.

On one occasion Los Angeles police were astonished to find presidential aide Murray Chotiner —once dubbed an "influence peddler" during the Eisenhower administration—living it up at La Costa while his boss, Richard Nixon, was at the Western White House, in San Clemente.

How did Eugene Hale Brading fit into this picture? Intelligence agents in the San Diego County Sheriff's office pictured the man they knew as Jim Braden as a gambler who participated in games of chance at La Costa and hustled gullible golfers for relatively small amounts of money. The FBI, as mentioned earlier, was particularly interested in his gambling activities as they related to Dallas.

La Costa had its fair share of gambling, probably to satisfy the old Las Vegas crowd. An intelligence report showed that there was a little casino in the country club's basement, with four roulette wheels, four blackjack tables, two pan games, and two keno games. Phones in the basement were used to receive "lay-off" bets from bookmakers. The bets, in turn, were sent by courier to San Diego, where they were reportedly handled by John Alessio's massive operation in that city.

Prostitution flourished at La Costa. Girls were recruited as far away as Las Vegas and brought to the country club to satisfy the needs of visiting dignitaries.

Such were the minor vices at La Costa, a natural carry-over from Las Vegas. But the Meyer Lanskys of organized crime usually played for higher stakes, and the central theme at La Costa was big money.

The first indication that the La Costa crowd was moving into Meyer Lansky's orbit came in 1957, when Frank M. Bogart, of Palm Springs, began making appearances there. Bogart had once been identified in intelligence circles as a "bag man" for Lansky.

On October 15, 1969, Moe Dalitz, Allard Roen, and Merv Adelson took off for Switzerland, ostensibly to raise money to be used in the movie industry. For some time investigators had had the feeling that "skimming money" from Las Vegas was being filtered back into the United States via the La Costa Country Club. Skimming, in the parlance of highrollers, is the art of hiding Las Vegas gambling revenue from the tax collector. Normally the money is removed from the casinos right after it is collected from the gambling tables and sent overseas—usually to banks in Zurich or Amsterdam—by a so-called courier, who can only be an elite member of the underworld. There can never be the risk of a double-cross. Usually the courier's fee is high, sometimes as much as 10 percent of the money taken overseas. After a period of time has elapsed—in some cases as long as two to three years—the money is brought back to the United States and invested in legitimate business activities. In the case of Moe Dalitz, the movie industry would be a "legitimate" investment.

Behind the scenes of all skimming activity in Las Vegas was Meyer Lansky, who held the combination to the cash vaults of the crime cartel in the United States. Lansky had operated Havana gambling houses for the syndicate prior to the time when Fidel Castro seized power. After that he moved to the Bahamas and then to Israel, where he sought refuge as a citizen when he became the subject of a massive investigation by a special "strike force" appointed by United States Attorney General John Mitchell.

There can be no doubt that Meyer Lansky was a genius, a man who quite easily could have made millions on Wall Street had he not chosen to throw in his lot with the organized underworld. The Italian Mafia feared him.

In October of 1971, while Lansky was fighting deportation from Israel, he was indicted by a Federal Grand Jury in Las Vegas on charges of skimming $36 million from the Flamingo Hotel between 1960 and 1967. That in itself was a record. Never before had federal agents come across anything like it. Lansky had masterminded the biggest coup in the history of Las Vegas—and the money was all out of the United States. Obviously Lansky had talent at his disposal; it had been years since authorities in Las Vegas had detected him on the Strip.

Moe Dalitz was one of Lansky's closest colleagues, and perhaps that explained the strange doings at La Costa, the appearance of Frank Bogard, and the trip to Switzerland.

Two high sources in the United States government, who knew I had been pursuing this investigation for three years, revealed to me that there was indeed a courier for the Las Vegas crowd at the La Costa Country Club, and his name was Jim Braden.

There it was again, popping out of the blue just as it did in Dealey Plaza. At first I was incredulous. Over and over again I had been told that Eugene Hale Brading was an accident of history, but now I had been alerted to his exact importance in the organized underworld. I was equally astonished when I was told that Brading was suspected of taking at least $72 million out of the country. One intelligence officer told me that was a "low estimate."

Until this information was revealed to me, I was somewhat hesitant about making public the information I had collected. Official confirmation that Brading was under investigation came from Robert Brosio, the number-two man in the United States Attorney's Office for the Central District of California.

Apparently the federal strike force got its first

inkling of Brading's suspected courier activities in the summer of 1971, when at attendant at La Costa opened Brading's golf locker for a routine inspection and found a huge sum of cash inside. Brading reportedly became furious and warned the attendant never again to touch his locker.

A law-enforcement officer personally connected with the investigation said that the amount of cash found in Brading's locker was believed to be about $120,000.

An intelligence officer from San Diego County told me he had actually counted the money and recalled the figure to be close to $200,000. But he said he was unable to determine if it was genuine or counterfeit.

In any event, most people don't leave six-figure amounts of cash in golf lockers. Brading told the investigators he obtained the money in an oil transaction. Indeed, he was connected with the Empire Oil and Regency Company, in Louisiana. But normally, money obtained in such a transaction would automatically go into a bank account, not a golf locker. One of the investigators who appeared to be knowledgeable about the case said he had obtained the information that Brading had been given the use of two planes owned by industrialist Howard Hughes. He speculated that Brading used the planes to carry cash out of Nevada. It was indeed another curious story about a very curious man.

Over the years Brading's activities continued unchecked for the most part, mainly because law-enforcement officers considered his background too demeaning for organized crime. Who ever heard of Moe Dalitz or Meyer Lansky being arrested for shoplifting or for bilking a wealthy widow?

But Eugene Hale Brading was a man for all seasons.

According to intelligence agents, the incident at the La Costa golf locker occurred in August of 1971. That October, the following story appeared in the "Around Town" section of the magazine *North County Living*, published in San Diego County:

Popular San Marcos resident (and La Costa Country Club member), Mr. Jim Braden recently wed Mariade Consuelo Iberra of Mexico City. The wedding took place in Las Vegas, Nevada with Mr. Victor E. Pereira and Mrs. Pereira in attendance. Returning to Los Angeles the Bradens hosted a large dinner party at the Petroleum Club which was attended by many friends of the couple in the North County area. The happy couple departed for a European honeymoon. On their return they will maintain residences at Lake San Marcos, Mexico City and Spain.

Eugene Hale Brading had come quite a way from his days as a "love bird" swindler in Dallas. Now, he was an item on the society pages.

EPILOGUE

This book was written over a period of four years, and during that time, after initially assuming the role of a skeptic, I gradually became convinced that the investigation into the assassination of President John Fitzgerald Kennedy must be reopened. And I am not alone in this conviction. Many of my journalistic colleagues who initially greeted the findings of the Warren Commission with satisfaction now share my belief that the final product of that investigation was at best a weak attempt at finding and isolating the truth.

It is my conviction that only a Congressional committee, armed with the power of subpoena, could adequately reopen the investigation. Such a committee would be able to obtain access to the scores of documents relating to the assassination of both John and Robert Kennedy—documents that have been classified by both the United States Justice Department and the Los Angeles Police Department and thus withheld from the public domain.

There are a number of difficult questions that a Congressional committee could seek to answer. Most significant, in my opinion, is: what role, if any did organized crime play in the assassination of President John F. Kennedy? There can be no doubt that the central figures in this book—Eugene Hale Brading and David William Ferrie —had documented ties to the organized underworld. Did in fact the "invisible government" of organized crime, which annually rips off millions of dollars from the American public, mastermind the assassination of the President who threatened to curb its power?

What role, if any, did paramilitary extremists play in the JFK assassination? Once again there is evidence that links the fanatical, assassination-prone Minutemen to the Mafia. Loran Eugene Hall, one of the great questionmarks in the Warren report, was indeed a member of the

Minutemen when he was unmasked several years after the assassination by the California Justice Department under his code name of Lornezo Pascillo. A Congressional committee might become quite alarmed if it broadened its investigation to include the Minutemen and their satellite organizations, such as the Secret Army and the American Volunteer Group.

Lastly, was the Garrison investigation in New Orleans, to be quite frank about it, a cover-up? In the year 1973 we Americans have become quite conditioned—through the eye-opening Watergate scandal—to believe in the possibility of governmental cover-ups.

Did David William Ferrie recruit Lee Harvey Oswald for a mission on behalf of Mafia chieftain Carlos Marcello? Why did Garrison refrain from identifying Ferrie as one of Marcello's closest associates and instead picture Ferrie as a right-wing extremist? Was in fact David Ferrie murdered because he was expendable in the eyes of the organized underworld? Why didn't Garrison make any mention of Eugene Hale Brading's presence in Dealey Plaza on the day of the assassination and instead tar Edgar Eugene Bradley with the brush of conspiracy when there was no evidence that would stand up in a court of law to place Bradley in Dallas on the day the President was murdered?

Why did Garrison repeatedly finger the FBI and CIA as conspirators in the JFK assassination? And what about Garrison's documented links to the organized underworld?

The American people deserve answers to these questions. Perhaps some day soon a Congressional committee will find the courage to ask them.

I feel confident that a reopening of the investigation would uncover a great number of facts and would bear out many of the documented statements I have made in this book.

But I would be completely satisfied if the only thing LEGACY OF DOUBT accomplishes is to clear Edgar Eugene Bradley once and for all of the stigma that resulted from the unproven charges made by Jim Garrison.

THE MOST POPULAR AND BESTSELLING NON-FICTION FROM PINNACLE BOOKS

THE SPRINGING OF GEORGE BLAKE by Sean Bourke. George Blake, a double-agent for nine years, working for both England and Russia, was in 1961 arrested, charged and convicted of blowing the cover of the entire Western network of agents in Europe and delivering to the Russians "every document of any importance which came into my hands." He was sentenced to forty-two years in Wormwood Scrubs prison. In 1966 his escape was engineered by the author of this remarkable book, Sean Bourke, a thirty-two-year-old Irishman who had been paroled in 1965 after spending over one-third of his life in jail. Bourke followed Blake to Moscow, where he was soon disillusioned. How he finally returned to the West, recovered the handwritten manuscript of the book he had been writing in Moscow, and eluded the British—who would even now like to return him to prison—makes a fitting climax to this true and breathtaking tale of our time. Critically acclaimed and widely serialized.

P00048-0—$1.50

IMPERIAL TRAGEDY, by Thomas M. Coffey. The true story of the first and last days of World War II, seen entirely from Japanese eyes. A battle tale, a diplomatic narrative, a study of Japanese society and culture—it is popular history in the best sense of the term—accurate, interesting and lively. From personal interviews given the author by people on all levels of Japanese life who were, somehow, involved in the attack on Pearl Harbor and in the atomic bombing of Hiroshima and Nagasaki. 740 pages, $12.95 in hardcover. **P00050-2—$1.95**

TIMES AND PLACES, by Emily Hahn. Welcome to the delightful, sparkling world of Emily Hahn, one of civilization's leading citizens and a writer of great wit and charm. In this book, she traces her colorful career as a journalist and world-traveler—from her youthful days in Chicago and New Mexico to her later years in Africa and the Orient. These intimate and amusing stories span almost half a century of round-the-world adventure; they make a most enjoyable voyage for any reader.

P00063-4—$1.25

To order see page 256

ORDEAL BY TRIAL: THE ALICE CRIMMINS CASE, by George Carpozi, Jr. The controversial Crimmins' case, a story still in the making! From a star reporter who was on the spot and in the know, here is the stranger-than-fiction chronicle of the sensational and bizarre Alice Crimmins' murder trial. The author's research uncovered startling new information which may lead to a new trial. The last chapter reveals—for the first time—new issues, new developments, new names . . . and a new motive for murder. Here is the life of Alice Crimmins and her tragedy-ridden family—and the seven men who formed an illicit web of love and intrigue about her.   **P00089-8—$1.25**

BURN AFTER READING, by Ladislas Farago. Here are the spy-masters, the heroes, the traitors, and all the cryptic subtlety and horrific violence that marked their grim activities. The more gripping because it really happened—it's all fascinating, particularly if you bear in mind that the same sort of thing is going on right this minute, as clandestinely and just as ruthlessly. By the author of GAME OF THE FOXES and PATTON. Fast-moving, smoothly written, yet fully documented.
                                    P00090-1—95¢

THE CANARIS CONSPIRACY, by Roger Manvell and Heinrich Fraenkel. An astounding chronicle of the plot to kill Hitler. This is the documented story of the work of Admiral Wilhelm Canaris' Department Z, pieced together from the accounts of survivors and told in full for the first time. This group attempted to liquidate Hitler in order to make peace with the allies, but before the plotters could achieve their goal, the conspiracy was discovered and broken by arrests, executions and suicides. One of the most incredible stories to come out of World War II.
                                    P00093-6—$1.25

DIVINE THUNDER, by Bernard Millot. This is the story of the kamikazes, the suicide pilots of Japan during World War II, and of why, when the need arose, they were ready to die without hesitation. In both soldiers and civilians, a mystical reverence for the homeland was almost second nature. The author describes their devastating assaults and the American reaction to them and he reveals what made the kamikazes men of such strange grandeur and heroism. With original drawings.
                                    P00108-8—$1.25

THE KENNEDY WOMEN, by Pearl S. Buck. Here are the fascinating and extraordinary women of the Kennedy family. With the skill of a journalist, the artistry of a gifted storyteller, and the seasoned eye of a biographer, Pearl S. Buck paints a portrait in words of the women who bear one of the most famous family names in history. From Rose, the durable and dynamic matriarch, to JFK's young Caroline—and including Kathleen, Rosemary, Patricia, Jean, Eunice, Ethel, Joan and Jacqueline—these are the ladies of our times.   **P00113-4—$1.50**

To order see page 256

STAND BY TO DIE, by A. V. Sellwood. The heroic story of a lone, embattled WW II ship. It was a small Yangtse river steamer, manned by a makeshift crew of fugitives. She sailed from war-torn Singapore to do battle with the armed might of a Japanese fleet. It was an epic naval action. Heroism was the order of the day. There were no lean British cruisers to divert the Japanese guns, there were no RAF planes to provide air cover. Just one bullet-riddled tub that wouldn't say die! The story could have been lost forever, as it has been for many years, had not A. V. Sellwood pieced together the almost unbelievable story of "the most decorated small ship in the navy."   **P00171-1—95¢**

SIEGE AND SURVIVAL: THE ODYSSEY OF A LENINGRADER, by Elena Skrjabina. A diary of one of the most devastating sieges in history. During the siege of Leningrad which began on September 8, 1941, nearly one-and-one-half million people died—of hunger, of cold, of disease, from German bullets and bombs. Elena Skrjabina survived. She endured. This book is a record of that experience, and it has been acclaimed by critics everywhere. *Publishers Weekly* said that it is "written in unadorned but eloquent prose that is remarkably effecting." *Bestsellers* said "It is human."   **P00199-1—95¢**

VIZZINI!, by Sal Vizzini, with Oscar Fraley and Marshall Smith. The secret lives of our most successful narc! Sal Vizzini may die because he wrote this book. He was formerly an undercover agent for the Federal Bureau of Narcotics—an assignment which took him to Naples, where he became a "friend" of exiled Mafia chieftain Charles "Lucky" Luciano; to Burma, where he blew up a heroin factory; to Lebanon, where he outwitted a Communist gun-running ring; and to Atlanta, Georgia, where he posed as a con in the Federal pen. He was shot three times, knifed twice, beaten nearly to death, and had several contracts put out by the Mafia to kill him. Many of the men now in jail will learn for the first time who put them there.   **P00226-2—$1.25**

WALKING TALL, by Doug Warren. The true story of Buford Pusser a sheriff who has become a living legend. Buford is an honest man, a good man, he has tried to clean out the criminal element of his community. In doing so he has been shot eight times, stabbed five, rammed by a speeding car, had his home fire bombed, and was trapped in an ambush that killed his wife. But, Buford still lives. He raided the prostitution houses, the gambling dens and illicit moonshine stills and almost single handedly ousted crooked officials. His story has been made into a major motion picture by Cinnerama.   **P00243-2—95¢**

BUGSY, by George Carpozi, Jr. The wild but true story of Benjamin "Bugsy" Siegel. By the time he was twenty-one, this handsome hoodlum had done almost everything a professional mobster could do. He formed the first gang of executioners for

To order see page 256

hire—the forerunner of the notorious Murder, Inc. It was Bugsy Siegel who transformed a sandy wasteland into Las Vegas. The same Bugsy Siegel who hobnobbed with Hollywood's royalty and was treated almost as a king himself. He wanted class and he tried to buy it at almost every opportunity. He traveled widely, ate in the finest restaurants, and owned an estate in Beverly Hills. His women were legion. But never far beneath the surface was a hard-eyed killer—a killer who died as violently as he lived.   P00244-0—$1.25

MICKEY COHEN: MOBSTER, by Ed Reid. Finally—the brutal truth about a well-known gangster! This is a story that Mickey Cohen would rather *not* have told, but a story that can no longer be kept secret. Mickey Cohen is a man who has always been larger than life, who is part of the social history of our time. He's a member of the Jewish Mafia, who has lived hard and lived flamboyantly; who brags about deeds most would want hidden; whose friends have been jet-setters, criminals, evangelists, film stars, politicians, and members of the Hollywood social scene. Right now, he's down but not out, and don't ever count him *out*! Not until the end.   P00257-7—$1.25

SUSAN HAYWARD: THE DIVINE BITCH, by Doug McClelland. The triumphs and tragedies of a fiery and talented screen star. Susan Hayward has lived a life to pale even her most vivid screen roles. The beautiful redhead was brought to Hollywood to test for the Scarlet O'Hara role in *Gone with the Wind*. She lost the part but established an acting career, eventually winning Academy Award nominations for *Smash-Up, My Foolish Heart, With a Song in My Heart, I'll Cry Tomorrow* and finally and triumphantly—the Oscar himself—for *I Want to Live*. In the interim there were two marriages, twin sons, and constant strife that persists to this day. She was a feminist before the fashion—with femininity plus and a drive to achieve that led her far from the Brooklyn tenement where she began her life. This is the first book ever on one of the First Ladies of the movies' Golden Age: Susan Hayward.   P00276-9—$1.25

INSIDE ADOLF HITLER, by Roger Manvell and Heinrich Fraenkel. This is *not* a book about politics. It is *not* a book about warfare. What is it then? It is a book about the mind of a man, a probing portrait into the personality development of the most hated man of the 20th century. **INSIDE ADOLF HITLER** is by two of the most renowned Third Reich historians. Their most recent books, *The Canaris Conspiracy* and *The Men Who Tried To Kill Hitler*, have sold millions. Here, for the first time, is an in-depth analysis of the public and private personalities of Adolf Hitler. The private Hitler, probably more than any other world figure, was totally different from what he was as a leader. Composed partly of reality and partly of legend, Manvell and Fraenkel attempt to separate the two: to dig behind the myth to find the human being.   P00277-7—$1.50

To order see page 256

This is your Order Form . . .
Just clip and mail.

_____P00048-0 THE SPRINGING OF GEORGE BLAKE, Sean Bourke ... 1.50

_____P00050-2 IMPERIAL TRAGEDY, Thomas Coffey ... 1.95

_____P00063-4 TIMES AND PLACES, Emily Hahn ... 1.25

_____P00089-8 ORDEAL BY TRIAL, THE ALICE CRIMMINS CASE, George Carpozi, Jr. ... 1.50

_____P00090-1 BURN AFTER READING, Ladislas Farago ... .95

_____P00093-6 THE CANARIS CONSPIRACY, Manvell & Fraenkel ... 1.25

_____P00108-8 DIVINE THUNDER, Bernard Millot ... 1.25

_____P00113-4 THE KENNEDY WOMEN, Pearl S. Buck ... 1.50

_____P00171-1 STAND BY TO DIE, A. V. Sellwood ... .95

_____P00199-1 SIEGE & SURVIVAL, Elena Skrjabina ... .95

_____P00226-2 VIZZINI, Sal Vizzini, with Fraley & Smith ... 1.25

_____P00243-2 WALKING TALL, Doug Warren ... .95

_____P00244-0 BUGSY, George Carpozi, Jr. ... 1.25

_____P00257-2 MICKEY COHEN: MOBSTER, Ed Reid ... 1.25

_____P00276-9 SUSAN HAYWARD: THE DIVINE BITCH, Doug McClelland ... 1.25

_____P00277-7 INSIDE ADOLF HITLER, Manvell & Fraenkel ... 1.50

TO ORDER

Please check the space next to the book/s you want, send this order form together with your check or money order, include the price of the book/s and 15¢ for handling and mailing, to:

PINNACLE BOOKS, INC./P.O. Box 4347, Grand Central Station/New York, N.Y. 10017

☐ CHECK HERE IF YOU WANT A FREE CATALOG.

I have enclosed $_____check_____or money order_____ as payment in full. No C.O.D.'s.

Name_____

Address_____

City_____State_____Zip_____
(Please allow time for delivery.)